WOODEN SPOON PUPPETS

By the same author
PUPPETS THAT ARE DIFFERENT

WOODEN SPOON PUPPETS

By

AUDREY VINCENTE DEAN

Illustrated by the Author

BOSTON   PLAYS, INC.   PUBLISHERS

First American edition published by Plays, Inc.
1976

Published in Great Britain under the title
WOODEN SPOON MARIONETTES

Library of Congress Cataloging in Publication Data
Dean, Audrey Vincente.
    Wooden spoon puppets.

    1. Puppet making.   2. Spoons.   I. Title.
TT174.7.D43   1976   745.59′22
75-28202
ISBN 0-8238-0204-3

Printed in Great Britain

CONTENTS

Basic Puppets   *page* 9   *Variations*

FAIRY   *page* 19   Angel, Princess

WITCH   *page* 24   Devil, Magic Broomstick

GRETEL   *page* 30   Gretel's Mother, National Costume, Schoolgirl

HANSEL   *page* 35   Woodcutter, National Costume, Schoolboy

FAT OLD KING   *page* 39   Even Fatter Old King, Prince Charming, Historical Character, Paunchy Old Dad

FAT OLD QUEEN   *page* 43   Schoolmarm, Fairy Tale Mother, Comic Cook

POP SINGER   *page* 48   Modern Young Man, Historical Character

GHOST   *page* 54   More Ghosts, Pianist

EXPANDING CLOWN   *page* 60   Normal Clown, Partners, Giant Clown, Tightrope Walker

BOUNCY BIRD   *page* 67   Other Birds, Bird of Paradise

DOG WITH FLOPPY EARS   *page* 74   Different Dog, Comic Horse, Cat

DRAGON   *page* 81   Dinosaur, Baby Dragon, Different Dragon

Puppet Theatres   *page* 86
Scenery and Props   *page* 88
Lighting   *page* 89
Suggestions for a Variety Show   *page* 90
Original Plays   *page* 91

MAN

Materials

Wooden Spoon, about 12 in long; 6 dress weights, each 1 in diameter; scraps of thick card; scraps of felt; undercoat; coloured enamel paint; thread for hair; impact adhesive. N.B. Any other form of lead, such as fishing, or curtain weights may be used, enough to make the body hang well and limbs drop vertically as soon as tension from strings is released.

TO PREPARE THE SPOON: Bore a small hole at the top centre of the bowl. Cut approximately $3\frac{1}{4}$ in off the handle so that it measures 6 in from tip to base of the bowl. Paint the back and the bowl of the spoon and 1 in of the handle at the bowl end with undercoat. Apply a top coat of enamel paint and add the features. See the separate section for ideas on how to do this.

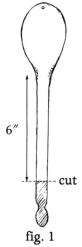

6"

- - - cut

fig. 1

BODY: Cut two pieces of thick card, each 3 in by $1\frac{1}{4}$ in. Round off the ends and mark the centre. Push the scissors point through the mark and rotate the blades until the hole is the right size to fit over the spoon handle. Push the first card on to the spoon handle and position it $\frac{1}{2}$ in below the base of the bowl. This forms the shoulders of the puppet. Secure

the card by winding string round the handle under the card and stick with adhesive. Make a small hole in each shoulder, $\frac{1}{4}$ in from the edge, for the strings.

The second card forms the hips. Fix two dress weights on top of the card at each end. Make holes in the card to correspond with the holes in the weights and tie them in position with string. Secure these and all other knots with a dab of adhesive. Curve a third dress weight with your fingers to fit the concave side of the spoon. The lead it is made from is quite soft and will bend easily. Stick it down and secure it by sticking strips of paper across it.

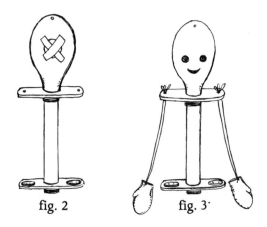

fig. 2   fig. 3·

HANDS AND ARMS: Cut out four hand shapes from felt in a colour to match the painted face, using the actual size pattern given on page 20. Oversew the hands together in pairs, leaving the wrist edge open. Cut a dress weight in half with scissors, stuff the hands loosely and insert half a weight into each. Close the opening. Double a 10 in piece of thin string and stitch the doubled ends to one wrist edge. Thread one cut end through the hole in the shoulder card and tie it firmly to the other end at the shoulder, so that the hand hangs with the thumb uppermost and the length of string between the hand and shoulder measures 4 in. Attach the other hand in the same way.

FEET AND LEGS: Cut two sole shapes and four uppers from felt, using the actual size patterns given on page 20. Stick the soles to thin card. Oversew the back and front seams of the uppers in pairs, then oversew the lower edge of the uppers to the soles. Leave the ankle edges open. Insert one whole dress weight into each shoe and stuff firmly. For the lower legs, cut two pieces of felt, each $3\frac{1}{2}$ in square. Stitch the edges together to form two tubes. Turn the stitching to the inside. Oversew one short end together, with seam at centre back, then stuff the legs firmly and the open ends to the ankle edges of the shoes, matching the back seams to the back seams of the shoes. Close knee edges. Sew the doubled ends of a 7 in length of string to the knee edges, and attach the other ends to the hip card through the holes in the dress weights. Adjust the length of the string so that it measures 3 in between the knee and the card, and tie the ends securely.

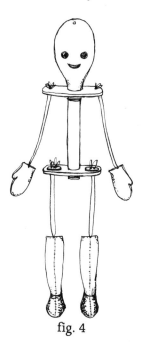

fig. 4

TO COMPLETE THE HEAD: Stick a pad of cotton wool to the back of the head to round out the shape. Make the wig and stick it in place. The separate section gives suggestions.

WOMAN

A woman puppet requires the same materials and should be made in the same way as a man up to the addition of the legs. At this point she may differ. If she is to wear long floor length skirts, legs are unnecessary. The puppet should, however, be weighted in the same way on the hip card and may need additional ballast to compensate for the lack of the leg weights enclosed in the feet. These can easily be added after the puppet has been strung. The dress may hang straight from the shoulders or it may have a full skirt, in which case you can cut the hip card 5 in by $2\frac{1}{2}$ in to support it. The extra measurements obviate the necessity for petticoats to give the top skirt volume.

CHILDREN

Child puppets can be made from smaller wooden spoons if they are to appear with the larger adult figures. Full instructions are given for boy and girl figures dressed as Hansel and Gretel on page 30.

If the children are not to be compared with other figures the proportion of the head to the body can be made a little larger by cutting a little more from the handle when preparing the spoon to make the tip to the bowl measure $4\frac{3}{4}$ in instead of 6 in. The hip and shoulder cards are cut the same as those of the adult.

FACES

Noses

If your puppet is supposed to be handsome or pretty, omit the nose altogether, but certain comic or wicked characters often look well when provided with some definite addition. Attach the nose before you begin to paint the face. The rounded ends of the sawn-off part of the handle may be useful. Drill a depression about half-way down the back of the spoon, remembering to hold the brace and bit at the angle you want the nose to slope. Cut the appropriate length from the handle and press

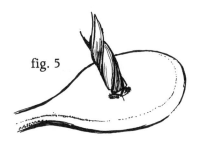

fig. 5

it in to the hole, whittling the cut end to fit the hole if necessary.

Noses pointing up are cheeky, downward slopes are evil. Forward jutting noses can support learned looking spectacles.

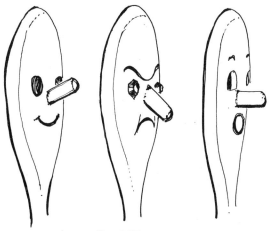

fig. 6 Noses

fig. 7 round nose

Another good nose can be made from a round wooden bead. Drill a small hole in the appropriate place on the back of the bowl and glue part of a matchstick in it. Press the other end into the hole in the bead, first wrapping a scrap of paper round it if it is too small. Glue paper over the hole in the other end of the bead to disguise it. You could use this nose for a clown or other funny men.

PAINTING: When any nose has been added paint the back and the bowl of the spoon and 1 in of the handle at the bowl end with undercoat, as mentioned before. Then add a top coat of enamel. Tiny tins of paint for decorating models can be bought from craft shops and colours can easily be mixed to desired shades, such as green-grey for a witch, pale brown tan for a pop singer, pink for pretty characters like the Fairy and Gretel.

Features

These should be painted neatly and accurately to look attractive. Use model enamel thinned slightly if necessary and a fine paintbrush. It is better to go over certain parts two or three times to make them sufficiently opaque than to paint them thickly in the first place and risk blodginess. Have a rag soaked in thinner handy to wipe away mistakes.

Do not try to be at all realistic when you come to design the features. The puppets will look more effective with stylized faces, which are easily painted. Circular eyes or pointed ovals should consist of solid colour. Do not try to add any whites at all. A comic pair of eyes can be white circles with two small squinting pupils. Other bulbous effects can be from two dome-shaped buttons, or saucer buttons with beads stuck in position. You can also buy joggle eyes for toy-making with loose pupils which slide about inside a transparent white.

MOUTHS: Let the mouth be simple new moon curves, turning up or down for smiles or frowns, or round dots the same size as the eyes for cherry lips.

EYEBROWS: Eyebrows can look startled or

frowning. Very slight wings can add to prettiness.

EYELASHES: These are features which can effectively be added to the painted face when dry. Trace them from the Identikit, fig. 9, and cut them from postcard. Snip into the curved dotted edges for eyelashes and curl each lash up carefully. To do this hold a pen knife in your right hand with the blade pointing towards the ball of your thumb. Grasp the card between the cutting edge of the pen knife and your thumb and with your left hand pull it through the pressure you are exerting. This very simple operation stretches one side of the card slightly and can be used on paper, card or gift ribbon. Stick the curved eyelashes to the face, which will need no painted eyes to suggest seductiveness.
Other eyelashes may be straight strokes painted round the eyes, for a more doll-like expression.

FRECKLES: Any country boys or young scamps may have freckles, about nine or ten small round dots in the hair colour painted over the nose area. Don't overdo them; otherwise your puppet will look as though he has the measles.

MOUSTACHE AND BEARD: These can be painted on, or they can be made from any hair material stuck on afterwards. Try postcard also for a more sculptured effect.
Suggestions are shown in the Identikit, fig 9, for various features following the above suggestions. An outline is given of the average spoon when it is laid flat or bowl side down. Slight variations in the size of the spoon you are using make no difference to the size of the features. With anything more drastic, scale the size up or down.
To use the Identikit trace the required features and assemble them in position on a piece of thin paper, then either use a carbon or scribble on the back of the drawing to transfer them. In general the eyes should be places half way down the back of the spoon. Variations in position will give interesting

results. Alternatively you could sketch in the features free-hand.

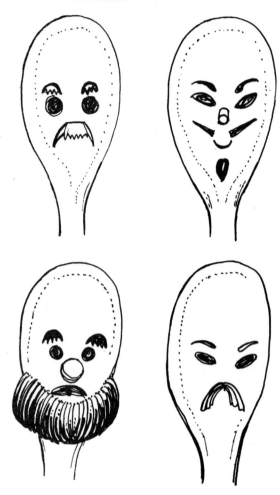

fig. 8 Moustaches and Beards

Hair
With every hairstyle, the important thing is to let the arrangement come well down over the front of the puppet's head. The average upper hairline is indicated by the dotted line on the basic spoon shape of the Identikit in fig 9. Any coiffure which drops round the face, such as the side wings of plaits or loose curls should cover plenty of the sides as well. At the back, the hair should cover the cotton wool pad inserted in the bowl of the spoon. The volume of any curls will increase the apparent size of the puppet's head.

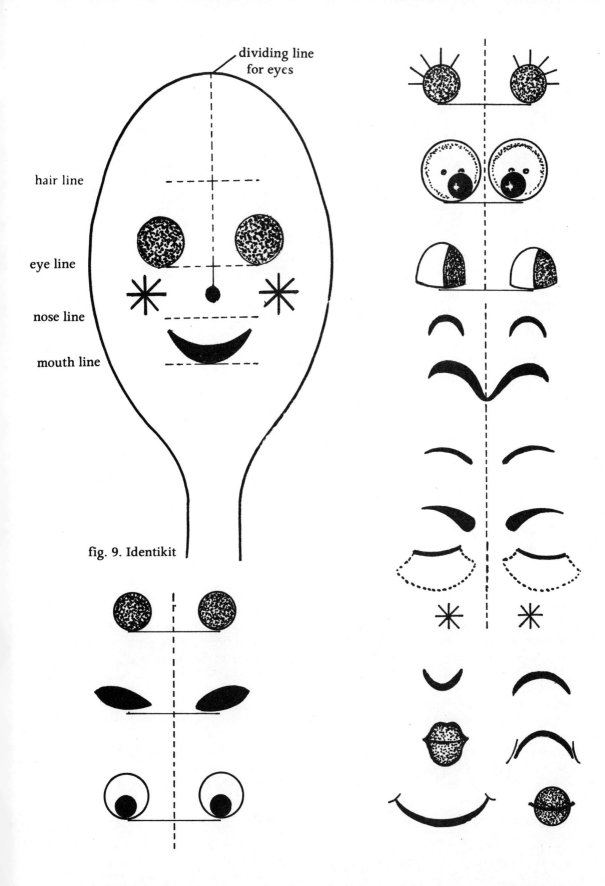

dividing line
for eyes

hair line

eye line

nose line

mouth line

fig. 9. Identikit

fig. 10

Because the cotton wool pad may show through the strands of hair if they are loose it is helpful to paint it to match with poster paint. Do not worry if, after having undergone its hairdressing, the puppet's head is still a little flat. As mentioned before, an attempt at realism is not desirable. Wool in its different colours is one of the most obvious threads for wigs. Synthetic shiny raffia, tubular rayon cord for macramé, curly metal panscrubber and wire wool are other suitable materials. Gift ribbon, curled as described for eyelashes would look wonderful as profuse ringlets. For a close cropped effect try fur fabric or felt. Natural fur or cotton will give an aged effect. With all the threads, the most obvious way to arrange the hair strands is to wind them round a book, back stitch up the page side and then cut them along the spine. The backstitching forms the parting. You can then trim the ends as you wish, arrange them in bunches, or plait them, enclosing pipe cleaners if the plaits are meant to stand out in a curve. For extra pieces such as a fringe sew a few more threads together and stick them in place. A bun can be stitched over all the ends taken to the back of the head. Solid ringlets are easily added by twining 4 or 5 lengths of pipe cleaner together and winding them round with the thread which has been used for the rest of the hairstyle. Stick the ringlets with the tops hidden by the rest of the hair and curve them becomingly. A wild curly effect can be made by closely winding double knitting or sport wool round a strip of wood, either straight or circular, with a circumference of $1\frac{3}{4}$ in. Thread a separate length of wool into a darning needle and back stitch all along the strands. Slip the wound length from the wood. Either make a little cap from felt or a cut piece of old stocking to fit the puppet's head and sew the wound lengths of hair to it in a spiral, starting at the centre back, or stick it straight on to the cotton wool pad. A spiral circumference of $1\frac{3}{4}$ in will give a medium length effect suitable for a girl or boy puppet. Narrower or wider measurements may be used. Let the hair come well down over the face and glue one or two curls over the cheeks.

STRINGING THE PUPPETS

This should only be done when the costumes and all the other details, with the exception of hats or headdresses, are complete. Female puppets without legs need only one control, but the male puppets need a second control to manipulate the legs. Any different controls are described in the instructions for individual puppets.

Control for Female Puppets without Legs
MATERIALS: A strip of wood 12 in long, 1 in wide and $\frac{1}{4}$ in thick (the last two measurements may be varied); a small cup hook; button or carpet thread in grey, black or brown.

To Make
Screw the cup hook into one end of the wood. Close up the hook a little with pliers and turn it so that the open end faces upwards. See fig 11. This hook carries the thread that supports the hands. Cut nicks each side of the control, 6 in from either end, and nicks at the end of the control opposite the hook.

To String
Thread a needle with about 24 in of thread and push it through the hole in the centre of the spoon head. Tie firmly. Take the needle in the correct place through any kind of head decoration and wind the other end of the thread round the nicks you have cut half way along the control. Knot the end. The length of the thread on which the puppet is suspended may be decided by the manipulator, but 20 in is convenient for an adult operating a puppet whose feet are on a level with his own. This is string 1.

String 2, the next to be added, is taken with a needle through the clothing and the centre back of the hip card. Tie the end. Suspend the puppet with your other hand from the control, ask someone else to hold it, or tie a piece of string round the balancing point and knot the ends in a loop so you can hang it on any convenient projection. Take the other end of the string up to the end opposite the cup hook and tie it round the nicks, adjusting the length so that the puppet is still upright. With the puppet still suspended, stitch the end of a 48 in length of thread to the upper edge of one hand where the centre of the forefinger would be. This is string 3. Take the thread up over the cup hook and down to the other hand (string 4). Push the needle through the imaginary centre of the other forefinger, adjust the thread length so that the arms hang naturally, then take one or two overstitches and tie the end. (See fig. 11a.) Secure all knots with a dab of glue and cut off excess thread.

Control for all other Puppets with Legs
MATERIALS: A strip of wood 12 in long and another 10 in long; a small cup hook; a 1 in dowel peg approximately $\frac{1}{4}$ in diameter

fig. 11

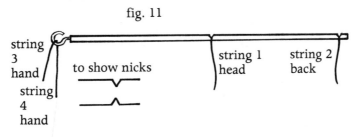

string 3 hand

string 4 hand

to show nicks

string 1 head

string 2 back

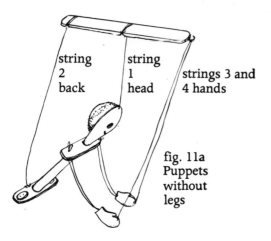

string
2
back

string
1
head

strings 3 and
4 hands

fig. 11a
Puppets
without
legs

(cut an inch from a piece of dowel); button
thread.

To Make

Insert the cup hook in one end of the 12 in
strip of wood. Drill a hole to fit the dowel peg
1 in from the cup hook end. Drill another hole
big enough to fit easily over the dowel in the
centre of the 10 in strip of wood. Cut nicks
in the centre of the 12 in piece, on either side
of the end opposite the cup hook and in either
end of the 10 in strip. Glue the peg in place,
using powdered wood glue or a contact
adhesive.

To String

Position strings 1 and 2 from the head and
back hip, as previously described. String 3,
which should be added next, is sewn into the
front of the upper leg at the knee. If the puppet
is wearing trousers make sure you go through
them and through the felt leg beneath. Put
the 10 in leg bar on its peg and suspend
the puppet from the main control, then take
the other end of string 3 up to the appropriate
end of the leg bar. Wind it round the nicks,
adjusting the length so that the legs hang
naturally, and tie the end. Treat string 4 from
the other leg in the same way. Lastly, add
strings 5 and 6 from the hands through the
cup hook, so that these will run on the outside
of the leg strings.

To Operate

Try to move the puppet smoothly and not too
rapidly. Tilting the main control up and down
will make the puppet raise his hands or bow.
A female puppet with long skirts can be
pulled along the floor, while you raise and
lower the control regularly so that it looks as
though she is walking. To operate the leg bar
rock the control from side to side while moving
it along, or take the leg bar off and hold it
in your other hand in front of the puppet,
rocking it from side to side while you bring

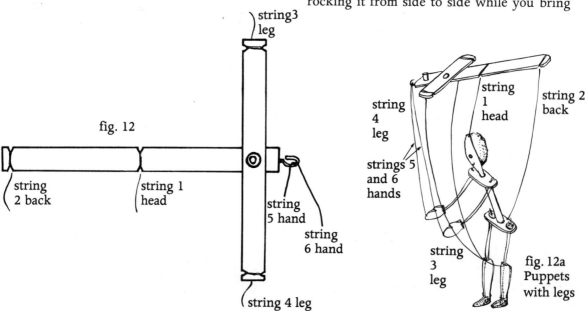

fig. 12

string
2 back

string 1
head

string3
leg

string
5 hand

string
6 hand

string 4 leg

string
4
leg

strings 5
and 6
hands

string
1
head

string 2
back

string
3
leg

fig. 12a
Puppets
with legs

the puppet along with the main control. Dancing is easy, so is jumping and flying. Practise effective movements of the hands and try to make your puppet perform in front of a mirror, to learn the most from your attempts.

FAIRY

The Fairy is an easy-to-make puppet. Her control is given two extra strings from the back of her dress so that it will not droop sadly when she is in mid flight. Make a separate removable crown from a three quarter circle of tinsel so that it slides over the head string and can be pinned in place.

Variations

1. *An Angel:* Make a white dress and white wings with crêpe paper feathers. Cut several of these at once by folding a strip of paper concertina fashion and making sure there is a connecting strip between each feather. Give her a harp instead of a wand.

2. *A Princess:* Omit the wings and wand.

FAIRY

Materials for Puppet
A wooden spoon; 4 dress weights, 1-in diameter; thick and thin card; thin string; white undercoat; pink, red and blue paint for face; skein shiny yellow raffia for hair; pink felt for hands.

Materials for Clothes
$\frac{1}{2}$ yard 36-in wide taffeta for underdress; $\frac{1}{2}$ yard 36-in wide silvery material, glittery chiffon or other suitable material for overdress; piece transparent plastic 6 in by 10 in, such as a gift box lid, for wings; white paint; sequins; beads; short length of silver Christmas tree garland for crown and wand; a lolly stick and silvery baking foil for wand.

To Make
BODY: Prepare the spoon as described in the general instructions. Paint the back and bowl and a short part of the handle for the fairy's neck with white undercoat, then give a pink top coat. Trace the fairy's face from fig 13. Paint the eyes in mid blue, the cheeks and mouth in red or deep pink. Cut shoulder and hip card and fix these in place. Make and attach hands and arms (page 9). Stick a $\frac{1}{2}$-in wide strip of stiff card between the shoulder and hip card to support the wings.

fig. 13 Fairy's face

19

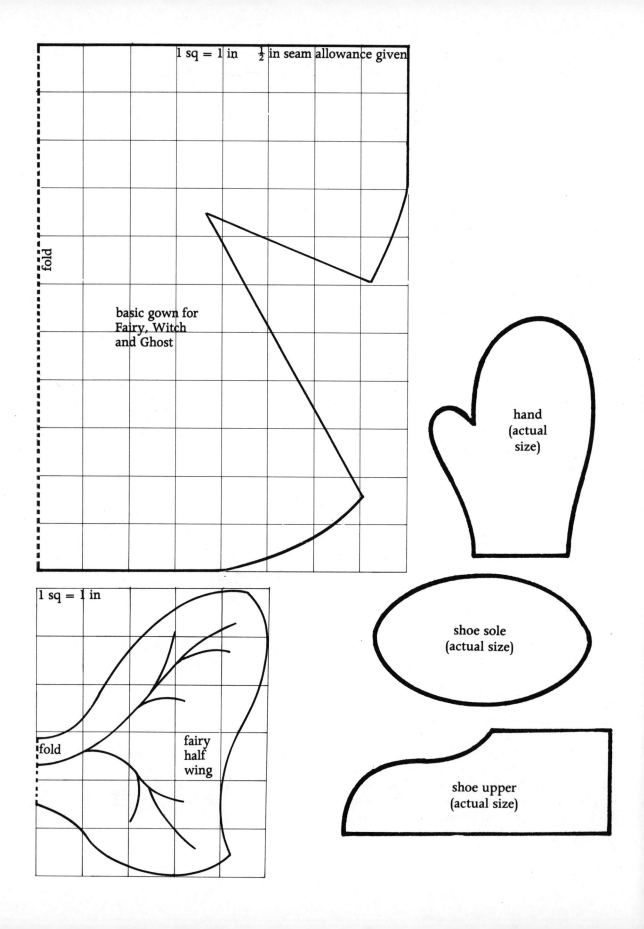

1 sq = 1 in   ½ in seam allowance given

fold

basic gown for
Fairy, Witch
and Ghost

hand
(actual
size)

shoe sole
(actual size)

1 sq = 1 in

fold

fairy
half
wing

shoe upper
(actual size)

fig. 14

HANDS AND ARMS: Make these up and attach them as described in the general instructions. As the fairy wears a long dress and has wings so that she can fly rather than walk, she needs no legs; but if you want her to have them, make up according to the instructions for the prince's legs on page 10.

Dress

UNDERDRESS: Make up the undergown from the basic pattern on page 20. Join the underarm and side seams, turn to right side. Narrowly hem the lower edge. Turn the neck edge in by $\frac{1}{4}$ in and run a gathering thread around. Slip the gown on the puppet and draw up the neck. Gather up sleeve edges and stitch to hands.

OVERDRESS: Cut out and make up similarly to the underdress, but do not gather the sleeve edges. Decorate with beads and sequins sewn here and there.

HAIR: Pad the back of the head with cotton wool and paint it to match the raffia, which should be wound round a book to give strands measuring 9 in long. from the parting. Back stitch along the raffia on one edge and cut the strands. Stick the hair in place with plenty of adhesive applied to the top and sides of the spoon. If the raffia is inclined to stick out apply adhesive between the strands and press them together, then tie a rag round the hair to hold it down and leave it for a day or two to set its direction. Trim the strands so that the hair is shorter in front than at the back and hangs decoratively over the shoulders.

WINGS: Cut the wings, following pattern, from transparent plastic and paint the veins as shown in white enamel, When dry decorate the wings by smearing the edges with glue and dipping them in glitter or else by sticking on sequins here and there. Working from the outside of the dress at the back, tack the wings by their narrow centre firmly to the card support.

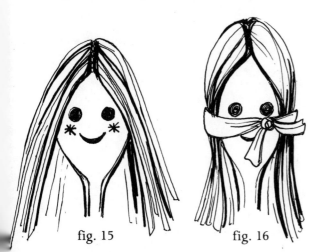

fig. 15   fig. 16

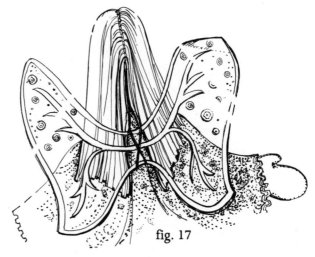

fig. 17

CROWN: Wind a short length of Christmas tree garland into a ring of about 2-in diameter and decorate with beads or sequins at the front. Stick or stitch it over the fairy's hair.

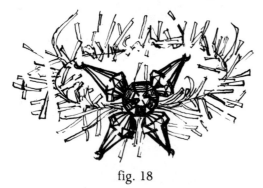

fig. 18

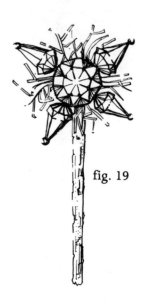

fig. 19

WAND: Split the lolly stick down the centre and cover with baking foil, add Christmas tree garland and beads to the top. You may thread the beads on to a short length of pipe cleaner. Stitch to the fairy's right hand.

Control
Make this in the same way as in the basic instructions for female puppets without legs. To make the fairy fly convincingly, attach a string to either side at the back of the skirt and tie them to the same nicks as the back string 2. In this way the skirt will not droop when the fairy is in the air.

The witch is an example of a female puppet with legs. These can be omitted and the witch can be given a long tattered dress. Make the hat removable by slitting it right up the back to the point after it has been sewn. It can then be slipped over the head string and pinned in place.

Variations

1. *A Devil:* Alter the colours of the witch's gown and hair to red and green. Omit the hat and make a pair of horns. He can carry a pitch fork.

2. *A Magic Broomstick:* Follow the instructions given on page 28. Give the broomstick a twiggy kind of face, as shown in fig 20. This can be cut from a piece of card. Leave a margin of about half an inch. Cut half-way into the margin and open out the card. Stick it on to the end of the broomstick and either paint it black or bind it round with thin strips of black crêpe paper. Add green

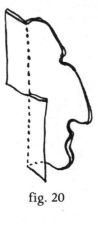

fig. 20

fig. 21

beads for eyes. Give the broomstick small twiggy arms by winding two separate thirds of a pipe cleaner with black crêpe paper and binding the paper in place. The control will be the same, but to make the broomstick hop about you will have to tilt the control until it is vertical and lift the top string.

WITCH

Materials for Puppet
A wooden spoon; 6 dress weights, 1-in diameter; thick and thin card; thin string; white undercoat; pale green, black and mauve paint for face; two flat-backed shiny buttons about ½-in diameter for eyes (optional); skein shiny mauve raffia for hair; pale green felt or cotton material for hands.

Materials for Clothes
½ yard 36-in fine emerald chiffon for underdress; ¼ yard 45-in chiffon for overdress;

piece black chiffon or fine material about 15 in by 12 in for cloak; 9-in square black felt and thin card for hat; small pieces black, emerald and mauve felt for shoes and stockings; sequins as you wish.

FOR BROOMSTICK: Piece round metal about $\frac{3}{4}$-in diameter, 12 in long; black crêpe paper to cover it and to make twigs.

To Make

BODY: Shorten the handle of the spoon, bore a hole in the bowl and stick the weight in it as described in the basic instructions. Saw a piece about $1\frac{1}{2}$ in long from the discarded part of the spoon handle for the nose; the rounded end will be its tip. Locate a spot in the centre of the face 2 in from the upper edge of the spoon bowl and drill a hole here at an upward angle to fit the nose, which should then be glued in place so that it slopes down.

Paint the back and bowl of the spoon, the nose and a short part of the handle for the witch's neck with white undercoat; then give a pale green top coat. Trace the witch's face from fig 22. Cut a round hole in the tracing paper where the witch's nose is indicated and fit it over the wooden nose when you transfer the features on to the spoon. Paint the mouth in deep mauve. The frown marks on either side of it, and the eyebrows, are black.

Stick the buttons to the face with impact adhesive for malevolent little eyes, or else paint black circles.

Cut shoulder and hip cards, weight the hip card and fix both in place. Make and attach hands and arms (page 9).

HAIR: Pad the back of the head with cotton wool and paint the cotton wool to match the raffia. Select a book about 6 in wide and wind the raffia round it, then back stitch the strands together along the page edge of the book. Do not cut the raffia. Apply plenty of adhesive to the top of the head and press the raffia on to it to resemble dishevelled hair; see fig 10.

HANDS AND ARMS: Make up the hands

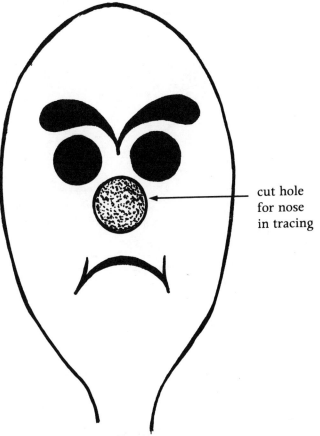

cut hole for nose in tracing

fig. 22 Witch's face

and arms as described in the general instructions, page 9, and attach them to the body. Use material if you cannot find felt to match the face, or use white cotton and paint it when made up in the correct colour with poster paint. In both cases allow $\frac{3}{8}$ in extra material all round for the seam. You may like to stick or sew mauve sequins on to the hands for finger nails.

LEGS AND FEET: Using the actual size pattern on page 26, cut 4 shoe uppers and 2 shoe soles in black felt. Cut 2 more shoe soles in thin card and stick them to the felt soles. Pin a pair of shoe uppers together and oversew from A–B and from C–D, turn work so that the oversewing is on the inside and pin the sole to the uppers matching A and C. Oversew the sole in place. Stuff shoes firmly, inserting a whole dress weight cut in two

25

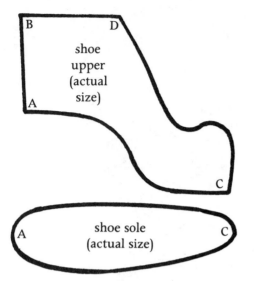

shoe
upper
(actual
size)

B   D

A

C

shoe sole
(actual size)

A   C

Attach the legs to the hip card as directed in the general instructions, page 10.

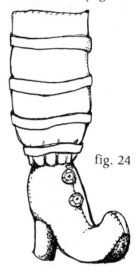

fig. 24

pieces into each, and lay them on one side for the present.

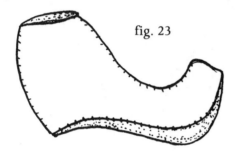

fig. 23

Cut 2 pieces of mauve felt, each $3\frac{1}{2}$-in square, for the lower leg; oversew 2 edges together on each and turn oversewing to inside. Gather one end of the resulting tube to shape the ankle. Stuff the legs and oversew the ankles to the tops of the shoes, matching the back seams of each. Close knee edges. Cut strips of emerald felt about $\frac{1}{8}$ in wide and stick them to the lower legs for horizontal stripes, catching them down at the centre back, or embroider stripes. For the heels of the shoes cut 2 strips of black felt each $\frac{3}{4}$ in by $1\frac{3}{4}$ in. Cut two $\frac{1}{2}$-in lengths of match stick and roll a strip of felt round each, oversewing the edges. Stitch the heels to the shoe soles. Finally add one or two sequins or beads to each shoe for buttons, or make silver buckles from pieces of card covered with baking foil and sewn in place.

Dress
UNDERDRESS: Use the basic gown pattern on page 20. Sew the underarm and side seams, slip it on to the puppet and gather the neck. Gather the sleeve edges and sew them to the hands.

OVERDRESS: Choose chiffon in dark shades for this; a mingled print of dark mauve, black, dark pink and so on would be splendid; purple or dark gold would also be mysterious. Cut 2 pieces 9 in by 7 in and 2 pieces 9 in by 14 in. Pin a 7-in piece to a 14-in piece, matching one edge, and oversew together for 1 in. Join the other pieces to them in the same way, alternating the measurements, so that the arrangement resembles fig 25. Now join

fig. 25

the first piece to the last piece. Turn the straight edge to the inside for $\frac{1}{4}$ in and run a gathering thread along. Slip the overdress on to the puppet so that the shorter lengths come over the underdress sleeves and draw up the gathering thread to fit the neck. Fasten it off. Catch the sleeve and side pieces together under

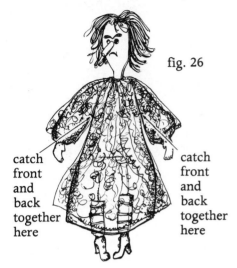

fig. 26

catch front and back together here

catch front and back together here

the arms. Suspend the puppet by a temporary thread put through the hole in the head and with your scissors cut or tear the overdress into strips so that the effect resembles the illustration on p. 23. Cut one or two bits shorter here and there and let the frayed edges show.

CLOAK: Run three gathering threads along one 15-in edge of the black chiffon, the first about 2 in from the edge, the second $1\frac{1}{2}$ in, the third 1 in, and draw them up to gather the edge to 5 in. Cut or tear the lower edge of the cloak into suitable tatters and arrange the gathered top around the puppet's neck. Catch stitch in place.

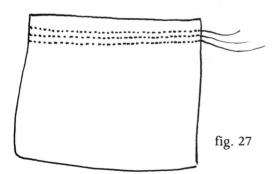

fig. 27

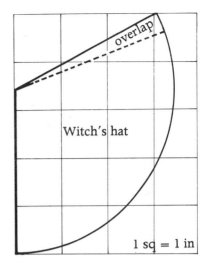

overlap

Witch's hat

1 sq = 1 in

HAT: Cut thin card according to the diagram above, and overlap to form a cone. See page 45. Cut the same shape in felt to cover the card and oversew the edges. For the brim, cut a 4-in diameter circle in thin card and mark a 1-in diameter and a 2-in diameter circle in the middle. Cut out the smaller circle and make straight cuts to the other. Bend up the resulting straight tabs and stick them inside the hat crown. Cut two 4-in diameter circles of felt with 2-in diameter holes in the middle and stick them over the hat brim, one under and one on top. Do not fix the hat to the witch's head until you come to string her control.

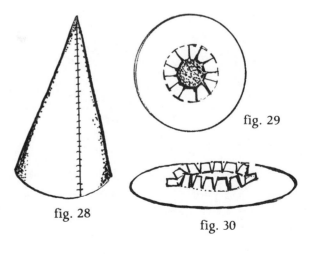

fig. 28

fig. 29

fig. 30

Broomstick

Cover the metal rod with black crêpe paper. For the twigs at the end roll spills of crêpe paper about 3 in long and arrange them round one end of the stick. Tie them in position.

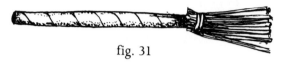

fig. 31

Control

Make this in the same way as in the basic instructions for puppets with legs.

Broomstick Control

MATERIALS: A 15-in strip of wood 1 in wide; button thread.

TO MAKE: Cut nicks at either end.

TO STRING: Attach strings at either end of the broom to the ends of the control. Adjust the length so that the witch can fly on her broom either sitting side saddle or astride it. The broom can be magic, as in *The Sorcerer's Apprentice* by Dukas, and move about independently.

GRETEL

This puppet is made from a smaller wooden spoon than the other puppets and the measurements are given to represent a child. Gretel and her brother Hansel make very charming folk dancers.

Variations

1. *Gretel's Mother:* Make on a full size spoon and add $\frac{1}{2}$ in on all edges of the clothes to scale the puppet to full size. Gretel can then become her own mother. Make the skirt mid-calf length.

2. *National Costume:* Copy the outfit from a book. A Dutch doll, with lace hat and sabots, would be a great success.

3. *A Schoolgirl:* Omit the bodice and make the skirt navy blue. Give her a school tie and scarf and a round school hat. She could also hold a school satchel.

GRETEL

Materials for Puppet
A small wooden spoon; 6 dress weights, 1-in diameter; thick and thin card; white undercoat; pink, red and blue paint for face; yellow wool or raffia for hair; pink felt for hands; black felt for boots.

Materials for Clothes
$\frac{1}{4}$ yard fine white nylon fabric; $\frac{1}{2}$ yard fine red fabric; $1\frac{1}{2}$ yards 1-in wide lace; 12 in patterned ribbon, approx. $\frac{5}{8}$-in wide; $\frac{1}{2}$ yard each narrow velvet ribbon in 4 colours; small piece of taffeta for apron; gold beads; small piece of iron-on adhesive material; scrap of black felt 7-in square; scraps of felt in different colours, including green.

To Make
BODY: Prepare and paint the spoon as described in the general instructions, but note that as the figure is a child the handle should be shortened a little more so that it will measure $4\frac{3}{4}$ in from its tip to the base of the bowl.

Trace Gretel's face from fig 32, and paint the mouth and cheeks in deep pink, the eyes in light blue and the eyelashes in grey. Cut the shoulder and hip cards and fix in place.

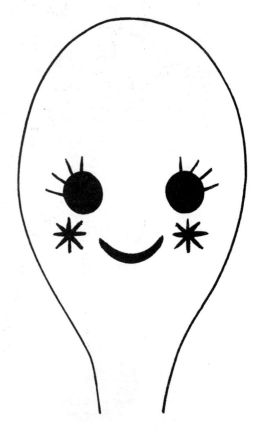

fig. 32 Gretel's face

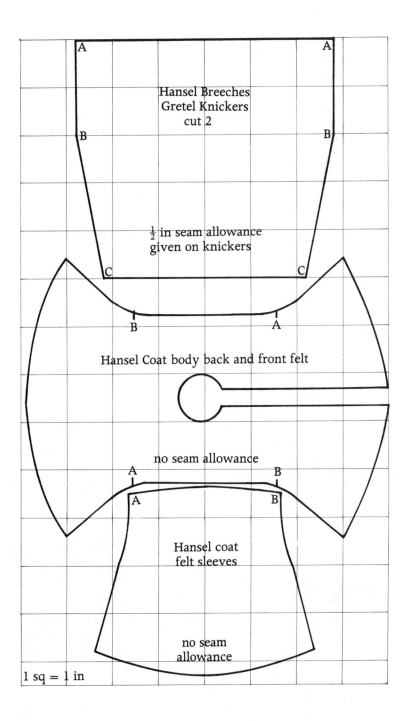

A   A

Hansel Breeches
Gretel Knickers
cut 2

B   B

$\frac{1}{2}$ in seam allowance
given on knickers

C   C

B   A

Hansel Coat body back and front felt

no seam allowance

A   B
A   B

Hansel coat
felt sleeves

no seam
allowance

1 sq = 1 in

Make and attach hands and arms (page 9).

HAIR: Make the basic wig by winding wool round a book as described for the fairy on page 21. Plait the strands together at either side of the head, enclosing a couple of pipe cleaners in each plait so that you can bend them outwards in a curve. Wind coloured thread around the plaits for ribbons. See fig 10.

BOOTS: Cut four shoe uppers from the basic pattern on page 20, and two shoe soles in black felt. Cut two squares of $3\frac{1}{2}$ in each. Make up the legs and feet as given in the basic instructions for a man puppet on page 10.

Dress

BLOUSE: Cut a piece of white nylon 9 in by 7 in. With right sides together join the two shorter sides. Turn to the right side. Turn in one raw edge for $\frac{1}{2}$ in and run a line of gathering stitches along it. Slip the blouse on to the puppet and draw up the gathers to fit the neck. Gather the other end slightly so that it fits under the hip card. Cut small slits for the arms and draw the hands through. Cut two sleeves, each 8 in by $5\frac{1}{2}$ in. Join the two shorter sides, turn to the right side. Turn in and gather one edge to approximately 3 in, slip the sleeve on to the arm and stitch to the blouse. Gather the other end of the sleeve and sew to the puppet's wrist. Attach the other sleeve in the same way.

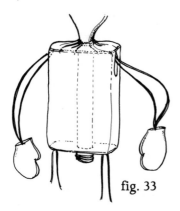

fig. 33

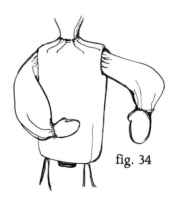

fig. 34

KNICKERS: Draw the pattern piece from the diagram on page 31, and cut out from the nylon fabric. With right sides together, join the first leg to the second leg from A to B for the back and front centre seam. Then join the legs separately from B to C. Turn to the right side. Slip the knickers on the puppet, turn in and gather raw edges and catch stitch at waist and knee.

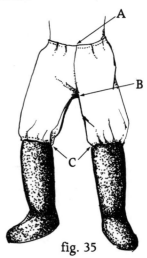

fig. 35

SKIRT AND UNDERSKIRT: Cut out a piece of red material 30 in by $5\frac{1}{2}$ in. Join the shorter ends. Turn a $\frac{1}{2}$-in hem along one longer edge and press a $\frac{1}{2}$-in hem along the remaining raw edge. Cut a piece of white nylon fabric to the same size for the underskirt and make up in the same way. Cut 9 in of lace and put it aside, join the short ends of the remaining piece of lace and gather it to fit the hem of the underskirt. Stitch in place around the hem. Slip the white skirt inside the red skirt, with the right side of the underskirt facing the wrong side of the skirt, and use a strong thread to work a line of gathering stitches along the top pressed in edges of the two skirts together. Put them on the puppet and draw up the gathers as tightly as possible. Catch stitch to blouse.

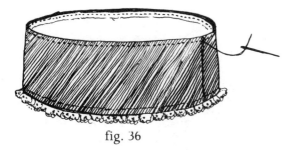

fig. 36

BODICE: Cut a piece of iron-on adhesive fabric $1\frac{1}{2}$ in by $6\frac{1}{2}$ in and iron it on to the red fabric. Cut out the red fabric around it, allowing $\frac{1}{2}$ in turnings all round. Press the turnings to the wrong side. Wrap the bodice round the puppet, overlapping edges for $\frac{1}{2}$ in down the centre back. Catch stitch the bodice to the skirt.

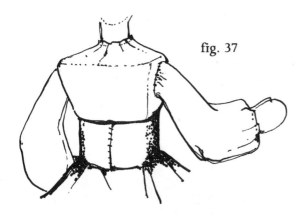

fig. 37

SHOULDER STRAPS: Cut two 6-in strips of ribbon and stitch to slightly wider strips of red material, pressing the raw edges of the fabric back and catching them to the wrong side. Position the straps so that the short edges are 1-in apart at the front waist, tuck the other ends inside the bodice at the back. Catch stitch. Couch down black thread to suggest the bodice lacing and sew beads at the outer points of the lacing.

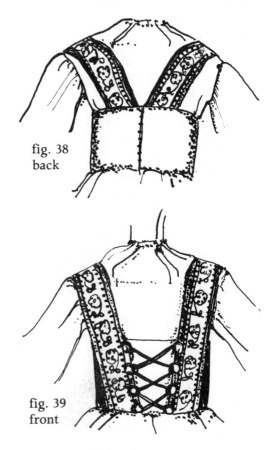

fig. 38
back

fig. 39
front

APRON: Cut a piece of taffeta 7 in by 8 in. Fold the taffeta in half along the shorter measurement with right sides together. Stitch along 3 sides and turn to the right side. Gather the top edge to $3\frac{1}{2}$ in and catch stitch to the front waist. Cut a long strip of taffeta 1 in by 20 in, and fold it in half along the length. Taking a $\frac{1}{4}$-in seam, join the long edges. Turn the sash to the right side, catch stitch to the apron and bodice, and tie round the puppet's waist to form a bow at the back.

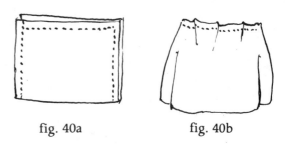

fig. 40a   fig. 40b

fig. 40c

fig. 41

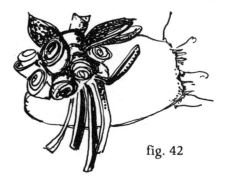

fig. 42

colours at each side of the top hair. Gather the remaining lace left from the underskirt to a 4-in length, join the short ends and sew it over the top of the ribbon loops. Position two strings of small gold beads at the front of the head dress as shown.

BOUQUET: Cut strips of felt approximately 4 in by $\frac{1}{2}$ in and roll up into cones. Stitch to secure. Make about seven flowers and stitch them together. Add narrow strips of green felt for stalks and leaves, and sew the bouquet to the puppet's right hand.

Control
Make this in the same way as in the basic instructions for puppets with legs.

HEAD DRESS: Cut the four $\frac{1}{2}$-yard lengths of velvet ribbon in two. Sew loops of all four

HANSEL

Hansel is the same size as Gretel.

Variations

1. *Woodcutter:* Make on a full size spoon and add $\frac{1}{2}$ in on all edges of the clothes, to scale the puppet to full size. Give him a removable beard. He could then become the Woodcutter in *Red Riding Hood,* and could hold a small axe, made from card and a small length of dowelling.

2. *National Costume:* Make a Dutch boy to go with the Dutch girl.

3. *A schoolboy, or a modern boy:* Make Hansel a pair of pink upper legs, each $3\frac{1}{2}$ in by $4\frac{1}{2}$ in. Oversew the knee edges to the knee edges of the lower legs, complete the stuffing and close the top. Attach a short string to the centre of each top edge and take it through the hip card. Make the breeches into shorts and either omit the jacket, or make a pullover to go over the shirt.

HANSEL

Materials for Puppet
Same as for Gretel.

Materials for Clothes
Remainder of the nylon from Gretel's dress; 10 in by $5\frac{1}{2}$ in piece brown suede, wash leather or felt; 9-in square of brown felt for hat; 12-in square of green felt for coat; a child's white cotton sock; 24 in velvet ribbon, approx. $\frac{1}{2}$ in wide; gold beads; $\frac{1}{2}$ yard patterned ribbon, approx. $\frac{1}{2}$ in wide; small piece of yellow felt for feather; 1 pipe cleaner; small piece of black felt for shoes.

To Make
Prepare and paint the spoon as for Gretel. Trace Hansel's face from fig 43, and paint the mouth in deep pink, the eyes in light blue, and the freckles in light brown.

HAIR: Make the wig by winding the wool round a book about 8 in wide and back stitching down the page edge. Before sticking the hair to the head give Hansel a fringe: wind wool about a dozen times round the first three fingers of your left hand, back stitch down the side of your first finger and slip the loops from your hand. Stick the fringe

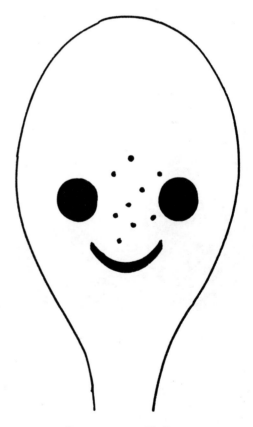

fig. 43 Hansel's face

to the centre top of the face, without cutting the loops, and apply some glue to the spoon so that the loops can be pressed on to it if they appear to stick out at all. Add the main wig to the rest of the head, placing the back stitching so that it appears to be a side parting. Smear some glue on to the sides of the spoon and the cotton wool padding at the back of the head so that the hair can be shaped with the scissors and then pressed into place. See fig 10.

SHOES AND STOCKINGS: Cut four shoe uppers from the basic pattern on page 20, and two shoe soles in black felt. Cut two $3\frac{1}{2}$-in squares of pink felt. Make up the legs and feet as given in the basic instructions for a man puppet on page 10. For the stockings, cut two pieces from the white sock each $3\frac{1}{2}$ in square. Wrap the white squares round the legs and stitch down the centre back. Catch stitch in place round the ankles. Shoe buckles may be represented by fastening a black thread to the centre front of the shoe and threading enough beads to form a small ring. Catch stitch at intervals round the ring to secure it.

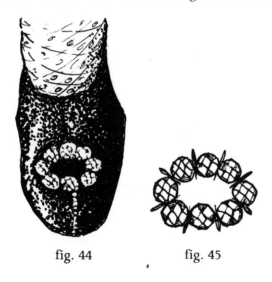

fig. 44   fig. 45

Clothes
SHIRT: As for Gretel.

BREECHES: Use the pattern for Gretel's knickers and make up in the same way. Add a strip of felt to decorate the knee edges.

BELT: Cut two 8-in lengths of red velvet ribbon and oversew them together down the long edges, with right sides facing. Open out the ribbon and stitch beads at intervals along the join on the right side. Wrap the belt round the puppet, overlapping it slightly at the centre back. Catch stitch in place over the top of the breeches.

NECK TIE: Tie the remaining piece of ribbon around the neck and stitch in place.

COAT: Redraw the pattern from the squared diagram on page 31. Cut the front and back and the two sleeves from green felt. Place the top edge of the sleeve A–B to the points A and B on the front and back and oversew. Repeat for the second sleeve. Fold the back and front in half along the shoulder edge, and oversew the sleeve underarm from wrist to armhole. Stitch side seam of jacket from armhole to lower edge. Join the other sleeve in the same way. Turn to right side. Sew ribbon round sleeve edges and down fronts. Slip the coat on to the puppet and catch fronts in place at the shoulder.

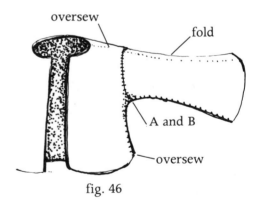

oversew   fold
A and B
oversew
fig. 46

HAT: Cut a circle of paper 4-in diameter and cut a 2-in diameter hole in the middle. This is the pattern for the brim. Cut out the brim in felt and cut another felt circle 4-in diameter for the crown. Gather the outer edge of the crown and draw up to fit the inner edge of the brim. Oversew the crown to the brim on the wrong side. Before placing the hat on the head, pass a long length of carpet thread through the front of the boy's hair and the hole in the top of the spoon. This is required for stringing and should be taken through the crown of the hat. Pad the crown slightly and stitch the hat to the puppet's head. To make the feather, cut a pipe cleaner in half and cut two pieces of yellow felt each 1 in by $2\frac{1}{2}$ in.

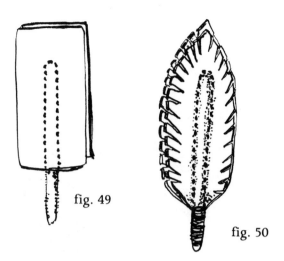

fig. 49

fig. 50

fig. 47 side

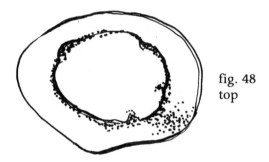

fig. 48
top

Leave about $\frac{3}{4}$ in of the pipe cleaner projecting, and enclose the rest with black running stitches down the centre of the two pieces of felt. Bind the ends of the pipe cleaner with black thread. Cut the felt to feather shape and snip diagonally into the sides. Stitch it to the side of the hat.

Control
Make this in the same way as in the basic instructions for puppets with legs.

FAT OLD KING

The fat old king is an example of a different shape of puppet. He definitely has a waistline problem.

Variations

1. *An Even Fatter Old King:* Make his waist card larger than the one given and adjust his shirt and breeches pattern accordingly. Give him a round red nose like the Expanding Clown's on page 60. Make his legs very short to add to the comic effect. To make a younger fat old king, remove his beard and give him more hair.

2. *Prince Charming:* Omit his waist card to slim him, and adjust the shirt and breeches pattern accordingly. Give him a short flared cloak to appear more dashing and alter his hairstyle.

3. *Historical Character,* such as Henry VIII. Study pictures of the period to vary the costume.

4. *A Paunchy Old Dad:* Elongate his trousers to full length and give him a jumper, cut from jersey material or even knitted specially.

FAT OLD KING

Materials for Puppet

A wooden spoon; 6 dress weights 1-in diameter; thick and thin card; thin string; white undercoat; pink, red and black enamel for face; small pieces pink, grey and black felt; small ball mohair or other fluffy wool; a little kapok; 2 shiny flat black beads $\frac{1}{2}$-in diameter for eyes (optional).

Materials for Clothes

4 in by 12 in piece satin or other suitable material for shirt; 13 in by 7 in piece of brocade for breeches; 17 in by 12 in piece velvet for cloak; $\frac{1}{2}$ yard of $\frac{3}{4}$-in wide braid for belt and knee decorations; fancy buttons for belt and shoe buckles; gilt chains and small Christmas tree ball for necklaces, or similar decorations; $\frac{1}{4}$ yard of gold braid for crown.

To Make

BODY: Prepare the spoon as described in the general instructions. Paint the back and bowl of the spoon with white undercoat, then give a pink top coat. Trace the face from fig 51, and transfer it. Paint the eyes and eyebrows

fig. 51 Fat Old King's face

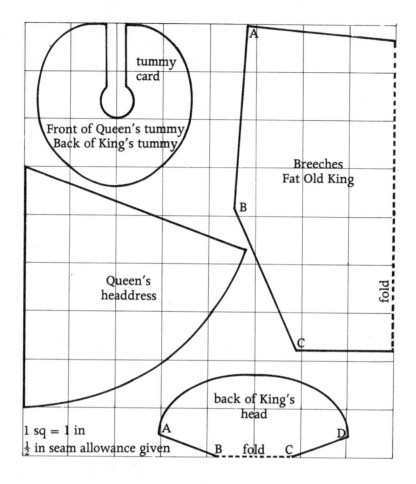

tummy
card

Front of Queen's tummy,
Back of King's tummy,

Breeches
Fat Old King

A

B

Queen's
headdress

fold

C

back of King's
head

1 sq = 1 in
$\frac{1}{2}$ in seam allowance given

A

B   fold   C

D

in black, the mouth in red. The eyes may be two black beads or buttons stuck on after the pink top coat is dry, to show up really well over the top of the beard. Position the shoulder card. Before adding hip card cut the tummy card from the squared pattern, using thick card. Make a hole in the middle and push it on to the spoon handle so that it is 2 in from the sawn end. Add the hip card. Stick and secure all the cards to the spoon handle, and weight the hip card. Make the hands and attach them to the shoulder card in the usual way.

LEGS AND FEET: Using the basic pattern given on page 20, and following the instructions on page 10, make a pair of shoes from black felt and lower legs from grey felt. Stitch decorations to the centre front of the shoes for shoe buckles.

fig. 52

BACK OF THE HEAD: Stick a weight to the back of the head and a pad of cotton wool over it. Cut the head back from pink felt, using the pattern on this page. Oversew from

A to B and from C to D and turn seam to inside. Apply adhesive to the inside edges of the felt and press it over the back of the head so that it sticks to the outside of the spoon.

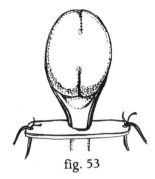

fig. 53

HAIR: Cut about 12 strands of wool each $3\frac{1}{2}$ in long and tie them together round the middle with a separate strand. Stick this bundle to the top of the head and clip it a little if necessary, to resemble the illustration on p. 38. Beard and ears are added last of all, when the shirt is in place.

Clothes

SHIRT: From satin or other rich material cut a piece 8 in by $12\frac{1}{2}$ in. Join shorter edges, with right sides facing, and press in $\frac{1}{2}$ in at top and bottom; then run gathering threads around. Slip the shirt on the puppet and draw up one thread to fit the neck. Draw up the other thread to fit under the hip card. Cut slits for the arms and pull the hands through, then complete with sleeves as for Gretel on page 27. Cut lengths of chain with pliers or old scissors for royal necklaces and catch them in place round the neck. Tie a gold Christmas bauble to the centre front of one of them.

BREECHES: Cut 2 legs from the pattern on page 00. Half inch turnings are allowed. Join the two pieces together on the wrong side from A to B at centre front and back, then join the pieces separately from B to C. Turn

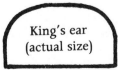

King's ear
(actual size)

fig. 54

fig. 55

to right side. Press in top edge for $\frac{1}{2}$ in. Slip on puppet and catch to waist, just around the tummy card. Cut a length of braid for a belt and stick in position, adding a few stitches, then sew a suitable decoration to the centre front to represent a buckle.

Turn in knee edges of the breeches to touch the top of the legs, and sew braid round the meeting point.

BEARD AND EARS: With mohair or other fluffy wool such as angora or bouclé used double, cast on 3 stitches with no. 1 needles (very thick ones). Working in garter stitch—plain knitting—increase one stitch at the beginning and end of each row until there are 15 stitches. Next row: knit 5, cast off 5, knit 5. Next row: knit 5, cast on 5, knit 5. Next row: cast off. Apply adhesive to one side of the beard and stick it to the face so that the upper edge comes just below the eyes, clipping the fuzz round the opening to that the mouth is clearly visible, and wrapping the sides round to the back of the head over the pink felt.

Cut 2 pink ears from felt following the actual size pattern and sew them to the sides of the head, just underneath the upper edges of the beard.

CLOAK: Cut a piece of velvet 14 in by 12 in and edge two long sides and one short side with gold braid. Run a gathering thread round the other short side and draw it up to measure 4 in. Cut a collar, on the cross if possible, $2\frac{1}{2}$ in by 5 in. Fold it in half with right sides together, and join the raw edges at each end with a $\frac{1}{2}$-in seam. Turn to right side. With right sides facing and raw edges together join collar to cloak, taking a $\frac{1}{2}$-in seam. Press collar up. Fold in $\frac{1}{2}$ in on remaining raw edge and stitch collar to the inside of the

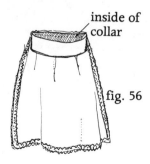

inside of collar

fig. 56

cloak. Catch the cloak in place round the puppet's shoulders.

CROWN: Join the short ends of a $4\frac{1}{2}$-in length of suitable gold braid and stitch the crown to the puppet's head after you have added the head string.

Control

Make this in the same way as in the basic instructions for puppets with legs.

FAT OLD QUEEN

This lady is a suitable partner to her husband. Notice that her waist card is turned round in the opposite way to the king's, to make her fat in feminine places. Her bust is a little bag, stuffed with cotton wool, and pushed up under her dress, pouter pigeon fashion.

Variations

1. *A Schoolmarm*: Dress her in navy and remove her head dress. Add a row of buttons down the front of her dress.

2. *The Mother in a fairy story*: Remove glasses and head dress and give her an apron.

3. *A Comic Cook,* such as the one in *Alice in Wonderland.* Give her an upturned nose, like the pop singer's, or a round red one, like the Expanding Clown's. She should wear a large apron and a mob cap, made from a circle of white material, about 6-in diameter, which is gathered to fit the head about 1½ in from the outer edge. A large wooden spoon, cut out flat from card or modelled from dowelling and papier mâché, will look well stitched in her right hand.

FAT OLD QUEEN

Materials for Puppet

A wooden spoon; 4 dress weights, 1-in diameter; thick and thin card; thin string; white undercoat; pink, red and black enamel for face; small pieces pink felt for hands; small amount of kapok; about ½ oz (14 grammes) of double knitting wool.

Materials for Clothes

15-in square of lurex or other suitable dress material; 18-in square of other material for underdress; 1¼ yards of narrow black braid; ¼ yard furnishing braid and fringe about 2 in wide to decorate underdress; 3 pipe cleaners and thin card for spectacles, black poster paint or Indian ink; thin card and gold paper for head dress; beads for ear rings; 6 collar stiffeners and scrap of chiffon or lace for fan; ¼ yard of gold braid for crown.

To Make

BODY: Prepare the spoon as described in the general instructions. Paint the back and bowl of the spoon with white undercoat, then give a pink top coat. Trace the face from fig 57, and transfer it. Paint the eyes and eyelashes in

fig. 57 Fat Old Queen's face

43

black and the mouth in red. Position the shoulder card, add the tummy card, noting that the curved edge is towards the back of the puppet, and stick and secure them all with the weighted hip card as described for the Fat Old King on page 40. Make the hands and attach them to the shoulder card.

No legs and feet are needed but if you decide to add them, make and attach them in the same way as the Fat Old King's or the Witch's (see page 10).

HAIR: Wind wool round a book about 9 in wide until the winding is about 4 in wide. Back stitch down one edge and cut the strands on the other side to the back stitching, then glue it to the head as a centre parting. Twist the sides into earphone buns and stitch them into place. Stitch drop beads under the buns for ear rings.

fig. 58

Clothes

UNDERDRESS: Cut the underdress 18 in by 13½ in, and with the right sides facing join the two shorter edges. Turn in 1 in on one end of the resulting tube and hem, then press in ½ in on the other end. Turn to right side, then run a gathering thread around the unhemmed end and draw it up to fit the neck. Cut two sleeves and complete as for the pop singer on page 50.

OVERDRESS: Cut a piece of lurex or similar material 13½-in square and with right sides facing join two edges. Turn up hem and top edge as for underdress. With seam at the back cut the front neck 2 in by 1¾ in deep as shown

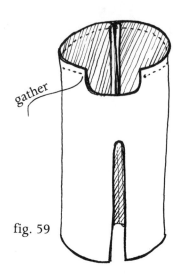

fig. 59

in fig 59, and oversew to prevent fraying. Slit centrally up the front for 8 in and press in edges for ¼ in. Trim on right side with the narrow braid. Run a gathering thread round the straight part at the neck edge and slip the overdress on the puppet, then draw up the thread so that the cut out neck sits well over the underdress at the front and the gathering fits the spoon handle. Catch the overdress and underdress together at the back of the neck. Catch front neck in place and stick braid round to hide edges.

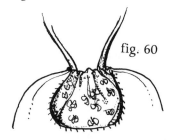

fig. 60

Cut slits for armholes and draw undersleeves through. Cut two oversleeves each 7½ in by 2½ in, join short edges with right sides facing and turn to right side. Oversew or narrowly turn in the other edges to prevent fraying and cover one of them on each sleeve with braid to match that on the dress.

Run gathering threads round the other edges and draw up to fit armholes, then catch over sleeves in place. Cut a circle of scrap material 5 in diameter, gather round the outside, and

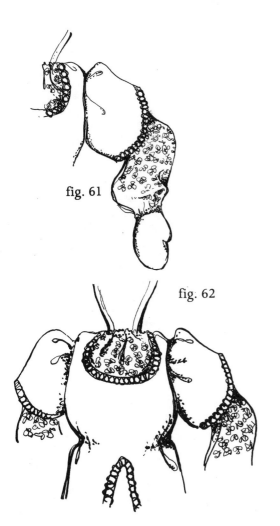

fig. 61

fig. 62

SPECTACLES: Trace the actual size pattern for the spectacles on to thin card and cut it out. If the result seems at all flimsy twist two pipe cleaners into rings to fit and stick them on the card for added strength, with another bit of pipe cleaner across the bridge of the nose.

Paint the specs black or some other colour, using Indian ink or poster colour, bend the arms at right angles and fasten them into the hair with a little adhesive.

fig. 63

HEAD DRESS: Following the pattern on page 40 cut one shape from card. To curve it, place the card on a table while you hold the edge of a ruler firmly over it at right angles.

fig. 64

insert stuffing before drawing up to form a little cushion. Stick this to the spoon handle beneath the underdress. It will suggest a portly bosom. Leaving approximately $2\frac{1}{2}$ in ungathered in centre front, run a gathering thread around the waist to draw it in slightly.

Pull the card slowly towards you from under the ruler edge. In this way one surface of the card is stretched so that you can easily curve it into a cone. Stick the edges down, overlapping them about $\frac{1}{2}$ in. Cut a piece of gold paper the same shape and cover the card with

Queen's Spectacles (actual size)

it. Cut a small piece of chiffon or veiling to hang from the tip of the head dress. After the puppet has been strung stitch the head dress to the head at a sloping angle, taking the head strings through it, and encircle the bottom of the cone with a length of braid to represent a gold crown.

FAN: Take 6 collar stiffeners and cut them down to measure 2 in if they are too long. Failing collar stiffeners use strips of card each 2 in by $\frac{1}{4}$ in. Roughen one end of the stiffeners by scratching them with the scissors point, and stick them into a fan shape, one on top of the other, with contact adhesive. When they are dry stick lace or chiffon over the top of the fan, and stitch it to the Queen's hand.

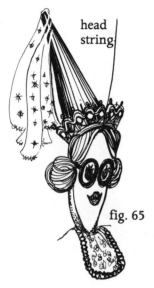

head string

fig. 65

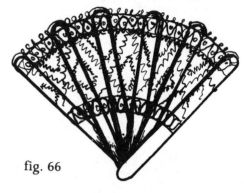

fig. 66

Control

Make this in the same way as the basic instructions for female puppets without legs.

The pop singer can do a turn of his own. Alter his clothes to suit the style of the moment.

Variations

1. *A Modern Young Man*: Make the hairstyle more orthodox, and give him a white or coloured shirt with a turn over collar and a tie. He can also wear a polo neck as given in the pattern. Remove the flare from the trousers and make them from tweedy material. Omit the guitar and sunglasses and the upturned nose and give him a face similar to Hansel's but without the freckles.

2. *A Historical Character*: such as Charles II. He will need a full wig, which can be similar to the one he has already. Shorten the trousers into breeches and add ruffles and ribbons. Put stockings over the lower legs and give him shoes like the pop singer or even like the witch.

POP SINGER

Materials for Puppet
A wooden spoon; 7 dress weights 1-in diameter; thick and thin card; thin string; white undercoat; pale brown, black and orange paint for face; pale brown felt for hands and legs; small pieces mauve and bright pink felt for shoes; approx. 25 grammes of 4-ply wool for hair.

Materials for Clothes
$\frac{1}{4}$ yard 36-in wide glittery material for jacket and trousers; piece of satin 9 in by 18 in for shirt; $\frac{1}{2}$ yard narrow sequin banding; small glittery brooch and length of gold cord for necklace.

FOR SUNGLASSES: 2 pipe cleaners; 2 black sequins or similar shiny black circles $\frac{3}{4}$ in wide; gold thread or paper to wrap pipe cleaners.

FOR GUITAR: Thick and thin card; black carpet thread; $\frac{1}{2}$ yard narrow gold braid; small pieces gold thick thread.

To Make
BODY: Prepare the spoon, but before painting cut a 1-in length from the discarded part of the spoon handle for the nose, having the rounded end for its tip. Find the centre of the

face 2 in from the upper edge of the spoon bowl and drill a hole at a downward angle to fit the nose. Glue it in place so that it points upwards.

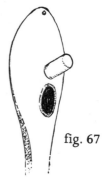

fig. 67

Paint the spoon with undercoat and give a pale brown top coat. Trace the face from fig 68 and cut a round hole in the paper where the nose is indicated so that you can fit it over the wooden nose when you transfer the features.

Paint the centre of the mouth in black and the lips round it in orange. No eyes are needed as they are obscured by the sunglasses.

Cut the shoulder and hip cards and fix in place. Make and attach hands and arms (page 9).

HAIR: Pad the back of the head with cotton wool and paint it to match the 4-ply wool. This could be coarsely crocheted, knitted or

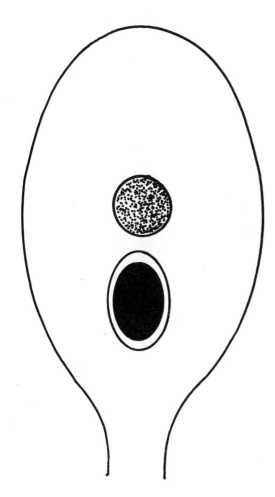

fig. 68 Pop Singer's face

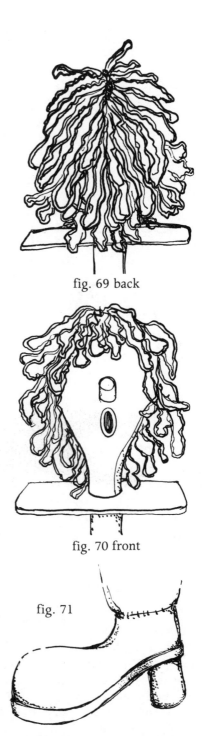

fig. 69 back

fig. 70 front

fig. 71

plaited, and may be worked double to save time. Press it well under a damp cloth and then unravel it. It will now appear wildly frizzy. Hold out your left hand with the fingers together and loop the wool round it unevenly, then back stitch it together down the side of your forefinger. Smear plenty of glue on the head and press the wool on to it, with the back stitching in the top centre of the head and the loops spread out around the outside of the spoon.

LEGS AND FEET: Cut two $3\frac{1}{2}$-in squares for the lower legs, and using the squared pattern on page 50, cut two shoe soles and four uppers from mauve felt. Make up the legs and feet as described in the basic instructions.

For the high heels cut two strips of lead about $\frac{1}{4}$ in wide by $\frac{1}{2}$ in long from a dress weight and two pieces of thin card $\frac{3}{4}$ in wide by 2 in long. Roll a piece of card round each bit of lead, and then roll pink felt round the card so that each

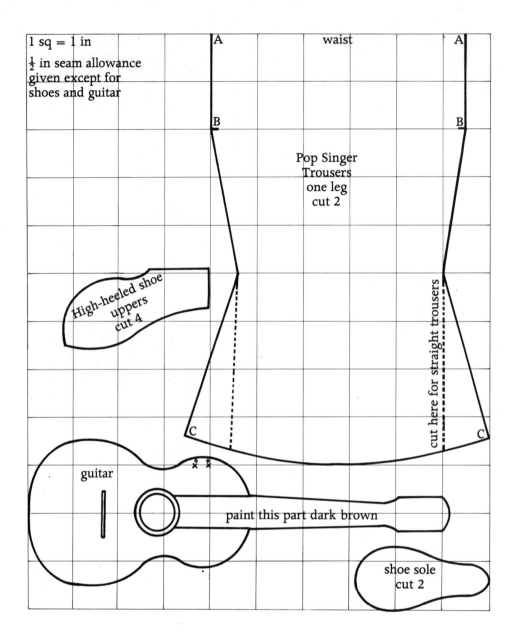

1 sq = 1 in
½ in seam allowance given except for shoes and guitar

A · waist · A

B · B

Pop Singer
Trousers
one leg
cut 2

High-heeled shoe
uppers
cut 4

cut here for straight trousers

C · C

guitar

paint this part dark brown

shoe sole
cut 2

heel is now ½-inch diameter. Oversew the felt edges, then sew the heels to the backs of the shoes and stick a narrow piece of pink felt ⅛ to ¼ in wide right round the sole edge of the uppers, to decorate them.

Clothes

SHIRT: Cut a piece of satin 9 in by 7½ in. With right sides together seam along two shorter sides. Turn to right side. Turn in raw edge for ½ in and run gathering thread along it on the right side. Slip the tube on the puppet and draw up gathers to fit the neck. Stick surplus under the hip card. Cut slits for arms and draw the hands through. See figs 33 and 34 on page 32 Cut two sleeves, each 6½ in by 5 in. Join along two longer sides. Turn to right side. Turn in the raw edges for about ½ in at one end. Slip sleeves on the puppet and sew the turned in edges to the bodice, gathering slightly. Adjusting the length, turn in raw edge and gather. Stitch to felt hands. Cut a crossways strip $2\frac{1}{2}$ in wide and long enough to fit round the neck; fold it in half and press with an iron, tucking in the raw edges for about $\frac{1}{4}$ in. Stitch in position to suggest a stand up collar. Cut crossways strips about 1 in wide, fold them in the same way and sew them round the wrists.

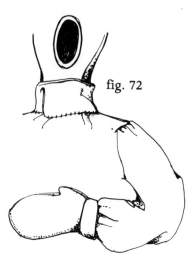

fig. 72

TROUSERS: A pattern for flared trousers is given in the squared diagram on page 50. $\frac{1}{2}$-in turnings are allowed. Cut two pieces the same. With right sides together, join first leg to second leg from A to B for front and back seams. Then join legs separately from B to C. Turn to right side. Turn in raw edges at waist, stitch sequin banding or other fancy trim down the outside leg line, slip on puppet and pin the waist band in place. Hold him in the air by his head so that his legs dangle freely, adjust the length of the trouser legs and catch stitch the turnings. Add a belt made from felt or fancy braid.

JACKET: Cut a piece of material 12 in by $7\frac{1}{2}$ in. Turn in the two shorter edges. Gather one long edge up to 9 in and neaten with a welt made from a strip of material cut on the straight, measuring $9\frac{1}{2}$ in by $1\frac{1}{4}$ in. Press in raw edges for $\frac{1}{4}$ in and fold in half lengthways. Stitch the welt to enclose the gathering on the jacket. Run a gathering thread along the other long edge of the jacket and draw it up so that it fits round the puppet's shoulders. See fig 73.

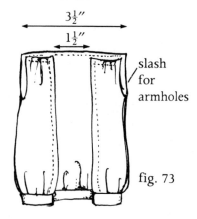

fig. 73

Note how the material is folded so that $1\frac{1}{2}$ in is left for the back of the neck and the total width across the shoulders is about $3\frac{1}{2}$ in. Slash down the side folds from the tip of the shoulders for about $1\frac{1}{2}$ in for the arm holes and neaten the back of the neck. Join the shoulder seams on the wrong side. Cut the jacket sleeves each $6\frac{1}{2}$ in by 7 in; join along the two shorter sides. Slash each for 1 inch from one end opposite the seam and oversew to neaten. See fig 74.

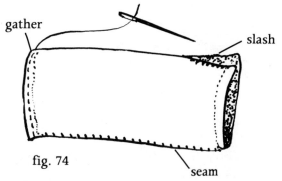

fig. 74

Turn in the lower edges of the sleeves for about $\frac{3}{8}$ in and catch down. Turn in the arm-hole edges for about the same amount, but slip one of the sleeves on the puppet first to adjust the length. Run a gathering thread round the sleeve top and draw it up to fit the armholes and give a puffed effect. Oversew the sleeves to the jacket from the right side. Slip the jacket on to the puppet and catch in position round the neck. Hang some kind of medallion or necklace round his neck.

fig. 75

SUNGLASSES: Cut two 4-in lengths of pipe cleaner and one $1\frac{1}{4}$-in length. Wrap each with narrow strips of gold paper or gold cord. For the lenses use two black plastic sequins or circles 1-in diameter, or cut two circles of thin card and paint them black. Apply glue round the outside of each circle and wrap the two 4-in lengths of pipe cleaner to surround them; join the two lenses by a bridge made from the shorter piece of pipe cleaner. Stick the sunglasses over the puppet's nose and push the extra lengths of pipe cleaner at the sides into the puppet's hair.

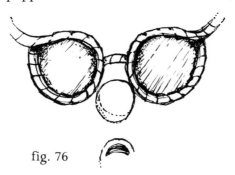

fig. 76

GUITAR: This is made from a thick piece of card painted as shown in the coloured illustration. The shape is given in the squared diagram on page 50. Make a small hook for the control string by bending a $1\frac{1}{2}$-in length of pipe cleaner in two and glueing the two ends behind the guitar at points x–x on the

squared diagram. Bend the pipe cleaner up at right angles to the card so that it makes a small raised loop. See fig 77. For guitar strings

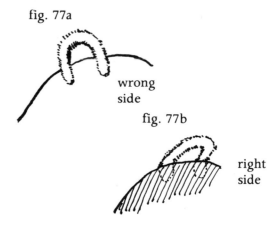

fig. 77a

wrong side

fig. 77b

right side

you may add lengths of black cotton, taken through the card at the straight bar in the main part and stretching up to the tuning knobs at the top. Glue the strings at the back of the card. There should be six of them in all. To weight the guitar, stick a dress weight at the back in the centre of the main part. Cut a 12-in length of cord and stick one end behind the top and the other to the centre of its base.

Control

Make this in the same way as given in the basic instructions, but let the string from the right hand go through the pipe cleaner hook you have fixed on the guitar, so that the puppet can strum the strings. Sew or stick the left hand to the top of the guitar.

If you prefer, you can omit the guitar and fix a small hand microphone in the puppet's right hand, made from a 2-in length of $\frac{1}{2}$-in diameter dowel or pencil tapered at one end. Cover it with black felt and sew or stick a small circle of white at one end. Add a long length of black cord to the tapered end of the microphone to represent the lead. The puppet's left hand will then be left free for appropriate gestures.

GHOST

The ghost makes the most effective arm movements with very little effort on the part of the manipulator.

Variations

1. *More Ghosts:* Paint the spoon back all over white and omit the skull details. Add two red or green glass 'jewels' or buttons for eyes. Drape a transparent winding sheet all over the ghost from the top of his head so that the eyes glare through it. Or dress the ghost in black, grey or white opaque material and omit the ribs. Or cut the spoon bowl entirely away from the handle, so that the ghost is just a head with a winding sheet draped over it. The hand strings can be single ones with a cup hook screwed into the control. Attach them to corners of the winding sheet.

2. *A Pianist:* Make and dress the ghost as one of the men puppets, but string the hands in the same way. He will perform wonderfully at the piano.

GHOST

Materials for Puppet
A wooden spoon; 4 dress weights 1-in diameter; thick and thin card; 10 pipe cleaners; opaque plastic bottle, white if possible; newspaper or tissues; wallpaper paste or flour paste; white undercoat, white and black top coat; 2 transparent or crystal sequins or two flat glass buttons $\frac{1}{2}$-in in diameter (optional); medium sized plastic bag.

For Undergown and Winding Sheet
Two pieces 9 in by 36 in fine white (or black) net; $\frac{1}{2}$ yard 36-in white chiffon or other thin white material; grey poster paint; $\frac{1}{2}$ yard medium weight chain.

To Make
BODY: Shorten the handle of the spoon and bore a hole in the bowl as described in the basic instructions. Stick the weight in place in the bowl of the spoon. Cut the shoulder and hip card and fix the shoulder card only in position. Paint the whole of the spoon, including the stuck weight, the handle, and the shoulder card with white undercoat and then with white top coat. Bore a hole to fit the spoon handle in the hip card and secure

the weights to it, as described in the basic instructions. Paint it with undercoat and top coat but do not fix it in place yet.

RIBS: Cut four $\frac{3}{8}$-in wide strips of plastic from the bottle as shown in fig 78, and trim them so that the longest measures 8 in and the other three $7\frac{1}{2}$ in, 7 in and $6\frac{1}{2}$ in.

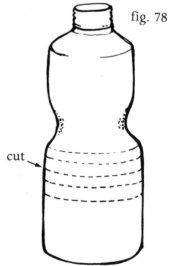

fig. 78

cut

Paint each rib on both sides with white undercoat and then white top coat if the bottle was not white to begin with. When they are dry, heat a needle and bore a hole in each end.

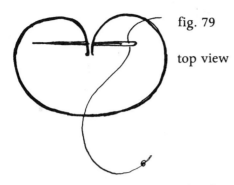

fig. 79

top view

Thread the needle with a length of strong cotton, and curl each rib so that it looks like fig 79. Push the needle through a matching pair of holes and tie the cotton so that the rib is held in shape. Cut off surplus cotton. Treat each rib in the same way. The joined parts will be placed at the front of the puppet. Turn the ghost so that the back of the spoon handle faces you, and make a mark $\frac{1}{2}$ in below the shoulder card. Make another mark 4 in below it. Apply contact adhesive to the centre back of each rib on the inside and stick the largest rib, measuring 8 inches, so that the upper edge touches the top mark. Stick the other three in descending order of size, evenly spaced, below the first one, so that the lower edge of the fourth rib touches the 4 in mark on the spoon handle. See fig 80. Contact adhesive must, of course, also be applied to the appropriate spots on the spoon handle.

Cut a $\frac{1}{2}$-in wide strip of thin card, 5 in long and stick it over the ribs along the back of the spoon handle, to keep them securely in place. If necessary you may also bind them to the handle with white cotton.

To Complete the Body
Slide the hip card on to the end of the spoon handle, with the weights downwards, and fasten in place by winding thread round the $\frac{1}{4}$ in or so of the handle which remains underneath it. Touch up the body with white top coat if necessary. Paint a fine black line, about $\frac{1}{8}$ in wide, round the edges of each rib. Trace the ghost's 'face' from fig 81, and transfer it; paint it in black, using a fine brush. When it is dry you may stick a transparent or crystal sequin shape, or a small flat glass button to each eye socket, to give them some glitter.

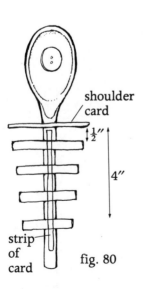

shoulder card

$\frac{1}{2}''$

4"

strip of card

fig. 80

fig. 81 Ghost's face

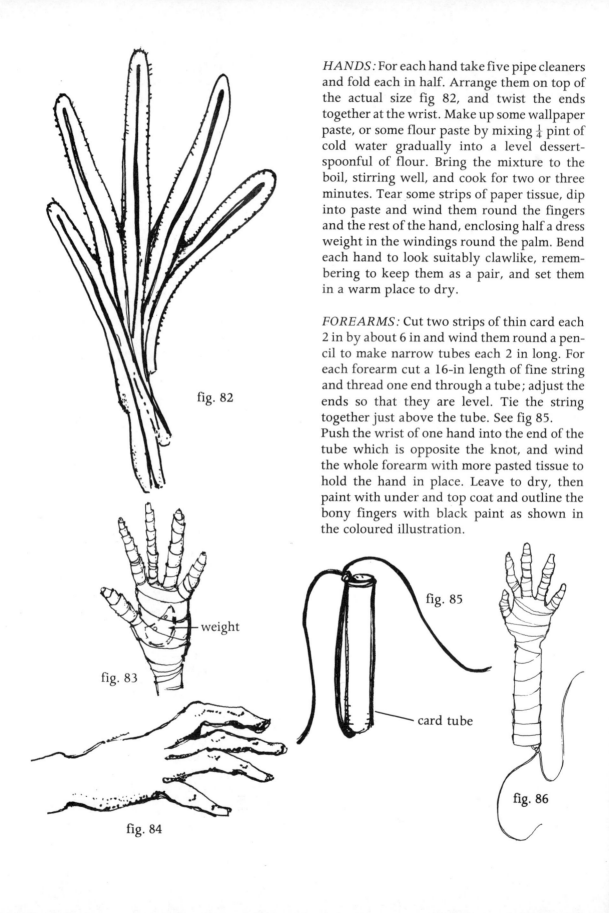

HANDS: For each hand take five pipe cleaners and fold each in half. Arrange them on top of the actual size fig 82, and twist the ends together at the wrist. Make up some wallpaper paste, or some flour paste by mixing $\frac{1}{4}$ pint of cold water gradually into a level dessert-spoonful of flour. Bring the mixture to the boil, stirring well, and cook for two or three minutes. Tear some strips of paper tissue, dip into paste and wind them round the fingers and the rest of the hand, enclosing half a dress weight in the windings round the palm. Bend each hand to look suitably clawlike, remembering to keep them as a pair, and set them in a warm place to dry.

FOREARMS: Cut two strips of thin card each 2 in by about 6 in and wind them round a pencil to make narrow tubes each 2 in long. For each forearm cut a 16-in length of fine string and thread one end through a tube; adjust the ends so that they are level. Tie the string together just above the tube. See fig 85.

Push the wrist of one hand into the end of the tube which is opposite the knot, and wind the whole forearm with more pasted tissue to hold the hand in place. Leave to dry, then paint with under and top coat and outline the bony fingers with black paint as shown in the coloured illustration.

fig. 82

fig. 83

— weight

fig. 84

fig. 85

card tube

fig. 86

UPPERARMS: For each upper arm cut a strip of white material 3 in by $4\frac{1}{2}$ in. Backstitch the short sides together in a $\frac{1}{4}$-in seam and turn to right side. Turn in one end of the resulting tube for $\frac{1}{4}$ in and run a gathering thread around. Apply adhesive to the top of a forearm and push the projecting string through the tube so that the gathered end may be slipped over the top of the forearm. Press the material in place, draw up and secure the gathering thread firmly. Finish the other arm the same.

Tie the strings to the shoulder cards as usual and adjust so that the hands hang with the palms facing the body and thumbs forward. Each arm should be approximately 8 in long from shoulder to finger tips. Gather the shoulder ends of the material tubes and sew them to the tops of the strings.

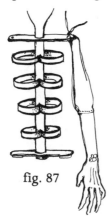

fig. 87

Clothes

UNDERGOWN: The ghost has no legs, as they seem superfluous if he is to float effectively, so to hide their absence he needs an undergown. Join the short ends of each net strip; one or both of these may be black if you prefer. Put one skirt inside the other and run a gathering thread along both edges at once. Draw up to fit the puppet's hip card. Apply adhesive around this and press the gathered net into position, then cut the undergown into pointed strips to give a suitably tattered and wispy effect.

WINDING SHEET: Use the basic gown pattern on page 20, but make it about 4 in longer. Join the seams by oversewing as invisibly as possible and turn to right side. Slip it on the puppet and gather in the neck. Cut the ends of the gown as before into tatters, and streak it with grey poster paint, applied with a large brush. Try especially to blend in the paint over the waist area so that the presence of the undergown and the absence of legs is not too apparent.

To Finish

You may like to add the effect of a vague shimmery cloud around the ghost's head, so to achieve this you can add hair, cut prosaically enough from a transparent plastic bag.

Scissor cut the bag into $\frac{1}{2}$-in strips, spiralling the cutting line so that you have a length of about 3 yards. Apply contact adhesive to the top, sides and back of the head, fold the plastic unevenly and press it into dishevelled lengths on to the head, adding more adhesive if necessary.

Drape the chain over the hands and tie it through the links, so that the ghost may rattle it in the time-honoured way.

fig. 88

Control

MATERIALS: Four strips of 1-in wide wood, 12 in, 10 in and two pieces 3 in long; one 1-in long dowel peg, $\frac{1}{4}$-in diameter; button thread.

TO MAKE: Drill a hole to fit the dowel peg 1 in away from one end of the 12-in strip.

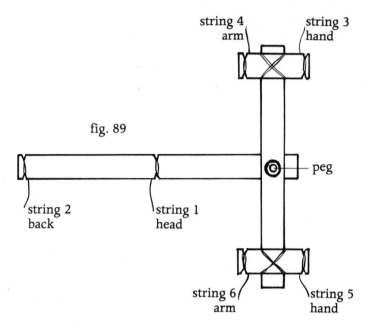

fig. 89

string 4 arm
string 3 hand
peg
string 2 back
string 1 head
string 6 arm
string 5 hand

Drill another hole to fit very loosely over the dowel peg in the centre of the 10-in cross bar. The play given to the cross bar by a large hole enables the ghost to move his arms freely while the control is still on its peg.

Cut nicks for the strings 6 in along the 12-in strip at the end opposite the dowel peg hole, and at each end of the 3-in crossbars.

Glue and bind the 3-in crossbar strips at right angles to the 10-in strip $\frac{1}{2}$ in away from each end.

Glue the peg in place.

TO STRING: Take string 1 through the hole in the head up to the nicks 6 in along the 12-in strip. String 2 runs from the back centre of the hip card to tie round the end of the same strip.

Tie string 3 firmly round the ghost's central finger, close to the hand. Suspend him by his control and place the 10-in bar in position on the dowel peg. Take the other end of string 3 up to the front end of the appropriate 3-in cross bar and tie, adjusting the length so that the hand is raised slightly. Sew string 4 to the inner bend of the elbow, where the material tube fits over the papier mâché, and tie the other end round the back nicks of the same crossbar. The ghost should now appear to spread his hand menacingly. Tie strings 5 and 6 to the other hand and arm, allowing them to have a different length so that the one hand is raised more than the other.

TO OPERATE: The ghost will drift about waving his arms menacingly, and rattling his chain, if you simply move his control while rocking it slowly from side to side. To raise his arms aloft in a curse or threatening gesture detach his arm control. He can fly convincingly. If you wish, add an extra two strings to the hem of his winding sheet as described for the fairy, so that the back will remain curved.

EXPANDING CLOWN

The expanding clown is a trick puppet and can provide a varied turn in a puppet revue. He can tap dance, do all sorts of contortions and acrobatics, and can grow in size out of his trousers.

Variations

1. *Normal Clown:* Make him in the ordinary way for a man puppet, so that he has a rigid backbone. Omit the heel and trouser strings, to simplify him.

2. *Partners:* Make two clowns, one tall and the other short and fat as for the Fat Old King. Use the shirt pattern for the King and the trouser pattern for the clown. Buy a joke book, or take notes from a television programme, and let them do a double act.

3. *Giant Clown:* Make the puppet taller still. Use very fine material for his shirt, such as silk or fine nylon, to allow it to fold down into his trousers.

4. *Tightrope Walker:* Sew a ring underneath one of his feet so that the end of a tightrope, off stage, can be threaded into it. He can then hop along the tightrope, while balancing a parasol or a column of balls.

EXPANDING CLOWN

Materials for Puppet

A wooden spoon; a round wooden bead about $\frac{3}{4}$ to 1-in diameter; 8 dress weights; thick and thin card; fine string; white undercoat; pink, red, black and white enamel for face; purple wool for hair; small pieces of purple and white felt; 2 flat buttons about 1-in diameter.

Materials for Clothes

Piece of thin scrap material 10 in by 3 in; piece emerald green corduroy 18 in by 15 in; piece flowered material 14 in by 9 in; piece red cotton 14 in by 9 in; small pieces lime green, orange and yellow felt; scraps of felt in other colours for patches; packet of pipe cleaners.

To Make

BODY: Following instructions on page 11 and fig 7, add the bead to the back of the spoon to suggest a round nose. Alternatively, a red circle can be painted in the centre of the face or you can stick on a domed button.

Paint the back and bowl of the spoon with

fig. 90 Clown's face

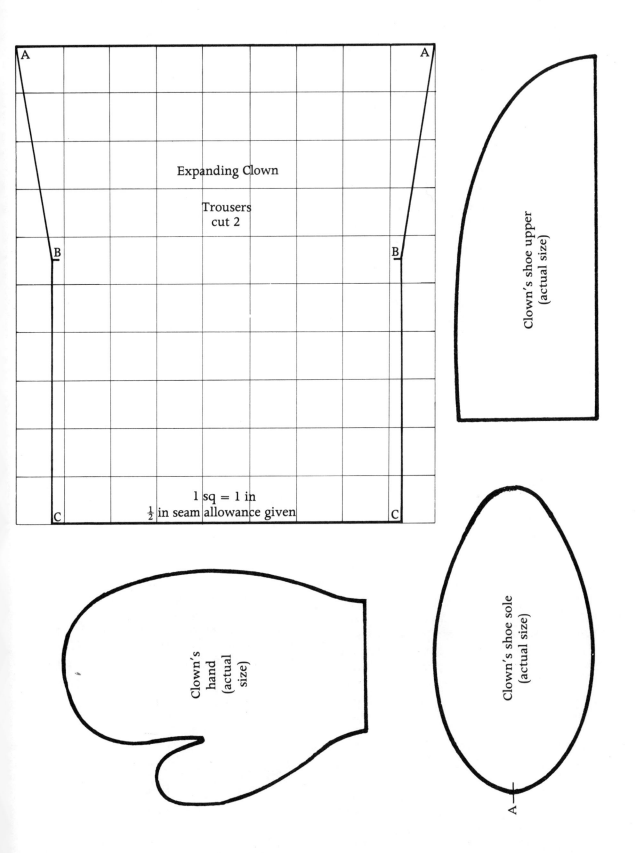

Expanding Clown

Trousers
cut 2

A

B

C

A

B

C

1 sq = 1 in
$\frac{1}{2}$ in seam allowance given

Clown's shoe upper
(actual size)

Clown's shoe sole
(actual size)

A

Clown's
hand
(actual
size)

undercoat and give a top coat of white enamel all over the back of the spoon only. Trace the features from fig 90, cut a hole in the middle of the tracing to fit over the nose and, after transferring them, paint the surround of the face in pink, leaving the white centre untouched. Paint the bowl of the spoon pink also. Add black eyes and eyebrows and paint the mouth and the bead or circle nose in red. Stick the weight to the back of the spoon and pad it with cotton wool. Saw off the handle so that only 1 in is left below the bowl, then saw $1\frac{1}{2}$ in from the remainder and set this aside for the present.

Cut the shoulder card, push it into place under the bowl of the spoon and wind string below to secure it as if it were the hip card. Make the hands from the special pattern on page 61 and attach them in the usual way.

Cut the hip card 4 in by $2\frac{1}{2}$ in, round the edges off well, push a hole in the middle and press it on the spare $1\frac{1}{2}$ in of the handle. Wind string above and below the hole and stick it to secure the card.

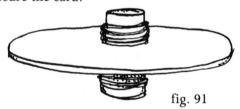

fig. 91

To connect the hip and shoulder card, take the strip of thin material 10 in by 3 in and join the long sides with a $\frac{3}{8}$-in seam. Turn so that seam is on the inside and gather the end of the tube to fit on the portion of the handle projecting from under the shoulder card. Wind the thread round several times to fasten it in place and glue to make sure the material stays put. In the same way fasten the other end of the tube to the piece of handle in the middle of the hip card, but before finally fixing it in place suspend the puppet by the holes in his head and make sure that the hip card hangs perfectly in line with the shoulder card.

HAIR: Make a curly wig by winding purple wool round a strip of wood or a ruler as

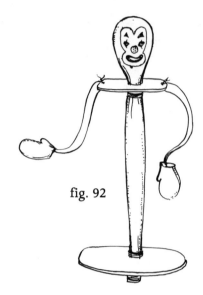

fig. 92

described in the basic instructions on page 14, and sticking it to the head.

LEGS AND FEET: Stick 2 dress weights on top of the hip card so that the inner edge of each touches the side of the spoon handle.

Cut 4 shoe uppers and 2 soles from purple felt following the actual size pattern. Cut 2 soles a little smaller all round than the felt from medium thickness card. Stick the card soles to the felt ones. Join the uppers down the straight centre back and the curved front seams, turn seams to inside.

Matching centre back seam to A join straight edges of uppers to soles, with card to the inside.

Apply adhesive to one side of each of two weights and stick them to the card sole inside one of the shoes, having one in the front of the foot and one towards the heel. Weight the other foot in the same way, then stuff each foot firmly. Take the flat buttons and stick

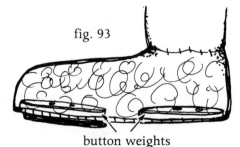

fig. 93

button weights

and sew one to the outside of each sole towards the toe ends so that the puppet can do a tap dance.

Make the lower legs from $3\frac{1}{2}$-in squares of felt in any colour, close centre back seam and knee edges and stuff. Oversew ankles to completed feet.

Attach the legs to the hip card with string as described in the basic instructions, page 10.

Clothes

SHIRT AND TANK TOP: Cut one piece 14 in by 4 in from the flowery material for the shirt, and one piece 14 in by 9 in from the red cotton for tank top, and join one long edge of each piece with a $\frac{1}{2}$-in seam. Open out the pieces and with wrong sides facing join them down the centre back into a tube. Turn work to right side and press in $\frac{1}{2}$ in at the shirt end. Run a gathering thread around it. Slip the shirt on the puppet with the seam at the centre back and draw up the gathering thread to fit the neck. Cut slits for the hands and draw them through. Hang up the puppet by a thread through the holes in its head, and, adjusting the length of the tank top if necessary, turn

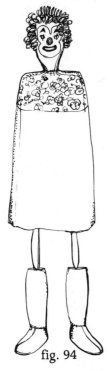

fig. 94

in the lower edge for about $\frac{1}{2}$ inch. Gather it and stick the surplus material under the hip card.

Cut sleeves $6\frac{1}{2}$ in by 5 in from the flowery shirt material and join along the two longer sides. Turn to right side. Turn in raw edge for about $\frac{1}{2}$ in at one end. Slip sleeves on puppet and sew turned in edges to the bodice. Adjusting the length, turn in and gather the other edges and sew them to the hands. See figs 33 and 34.

TROUSERS: A pattern for the trousers, including $\frac{1}{2}$-in turnings, is given on page 61. Cut two identical pieces from emerald green corduroy, remembering to have the nap or pile running the same way along each leg. With right sides together join each leg from A to B for the centre front seam. Then pin each leg together matching B to C on each piece and join these for the front and back seam. Turn $\frac{1}{2}$ in to wrong side at the lower end of each trouser leg and oversew.

To stiffen the waist of the trousers so that it will stand away from the body, twist two pipe cleaners together for about 1 in at the ends. Do the same to another two and then twist the total lengths together into a double thickness. Pin and tack the waist edge of the trousers over the pipe cleaners so that they are enclosed in a casing about $\frac{1}{2}$ in wide. Cut off any surplus. Machine stitch close to the covered cleaners.

Stitch patches in various colours here and there on the trouser legs, using thick yellow embroidery thread.

BRACES: Cut two braces each 18 in by $\frac{3}{4}$ in. If you are using thinner material than corduroy cut each 18 in by $1\frac{1}{2}$ in and fold in two lengthways. Oversew the edges to prevent fraying.

Sew one end of each brace to the waist edge of the trousers front, 1 in away from the centre seam on either side. You may like to stitch a big button on top of the ends.

Slip the trousers on the puppet and hang him up by his head cord. Take the braces up over his shoulders and cross them at centre back, then stitch the other ends to the back waist. So that the braces will not slip off his shoulders when the puppet is tucked into his trouser top, oversew the braces on either side to the shirt and tank top, starting about $1\frac{1}{2}$ in away from the waist.

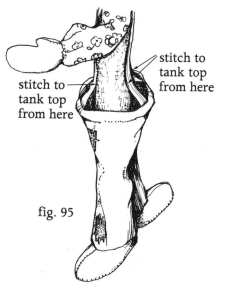

fig. 95

HAT: Cut a piece of thin card 5 in by $1\frac{1}{4}$ in and a piece of lime green felt 5 in by $1\frac{1}{2}$ in. Stick the short ends of the card together, overlapping them a little. Cover it with the felt and oversew the ends. Cut a round of felt to fit the top of the hat and oversew it.

For the brim, cut a circle of felt 2 in wide and cut a circle $1\frac{1}{2}$-in diameter from the centre. Catch the brim to the crown of the hat from underneath.

fig. 96

Cut a flower from yellow felt about 1-in diameter and an orange circle $\frac{1}{2}$-in diameter for the centre. Stick the circle to the flower and sew a gold sequin or small button in the middle. Stick the flower to the centre front of the hat and stick the hat to the head, after you have added the head string.

Cut and stick a similar flower $1\frac{1}{2}$-in diameter to the front of the tank top.

Control

MATERIALS: Four strips of 1-in wide wood, 12 in, 10 in, 7 in and 5 in long; 1 small cup hook; three 1-in dowel pegs, $\frac{1}{4}$-in diameter; button thread.

TO MAKE: Insert a cup hook into one end of the 12-in strip of wood and drill holes to fit the dowel pegs 1 in, $3\frac{1}{2}$ in and $8\frac{1}{2}$ in away from the cup hook end. Drill 2 small holes to take button thread each 3 in and 9 in away from the cup hook end. Drill holes to fit comfortably over the dowel pegs in the centre of the 10-in crossbar and 1 in away from both ends of the 7-in crossbar. Make sure that these last two holes will correspond with the dowel pegs in the middle of the 12-in strip of wood.

Cut nicks for strings 6 in along the 12-in strip, at the end opposite the cup hook and at each end of all three crossbars.

Glue and bind the 5-in crossbar at right angles to the 12-in strip 1 in away from the end. Glue the pegs in place.

TO STRING: Take string 1 through the hole in the puppet's head and through his hat up to the nicks 6 in along the 12-in strip. Fasten the hat to the head. String 2 runs from the back centre of the hip card to tie round the end of the same strip. Strings 3 and 4 come from the front knees to the ends of the 10-in cross bar. Sew the end of string 5 to one hand in the place where the centre of the forefinger would be and take it up through the cup hook to the same place on the other hand, so that it becomes string 6. Take strings 7 and 8 from the back of the heels to the ends of the 5-in cross bar tied on to the end of the 12-in strip.

The trousers are controlled by the 7-in bar.

In the diagram, the labels read:
"stitch to tank top from here" and "stitch to tank top from here"

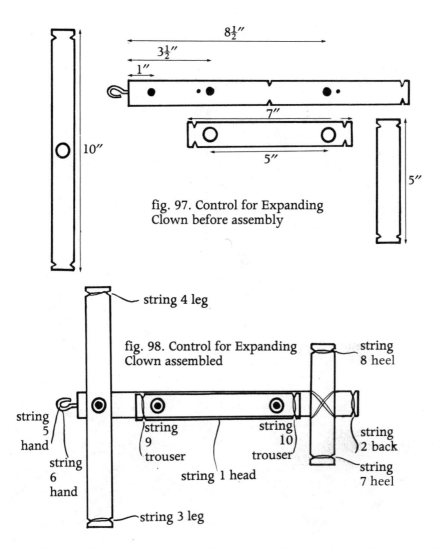

fig. 97. Control for Expanding
Clown before assembly

fig. 98. Control for Expanding
Clown assembled

string 4 leg

string
8 heel

string
5
hand

string
9
trouser

string
10
trouser

string
2 back

string
6
hand

string 1 head

string
7 heel

string 3 leg

Take string 9 from the centre back of the trousers waist band and run it up through the small hole in the main strip drilled near the heel cross bar. Suspend the puppet by his control and tie the trouser string 9 to the end of the trouser bar so that the trouser control can be held on the pegs while the trousers are held up by the string. String 10 runs from the front of the trousers and is fastened in the same way.

TO OPERATE: To make the puppet grow when he comes on stage push his body right down to the armpits into his trouser top and hold him up by his detachable trouser bar only. In front of the audience you can bring up his main control towards the trouser bar so that it will finally rest on its pegs when the puppet is fully extended, while you make suitable noises.

Your clown can do handstands while you tip up the end of his control and gather up the heel strings with your free hand. Other contortions are possible. The buttons under his toes enable him to perform a lively tap dance while you operate his detachable leg bar.

Pass one of his hand strings through a coloured card tube or one or two large beads to represent balls, and let them down from his control so that he appears to catch and balance them.

BOUNCY BIRD

The bouncy bird is easy to make and the greatest of fun to operate. He would also look well as a room decoration.

Variations

1. *Other varieties of bird:* Though he will still be comical, choice of different colours of felt will definitely turn the bouncy bird into different species. Try him in blues with a pink beak for a love bird, black and white for a magpie, brown for a thrush or yellow for a duck. Make up a play about a bird who lives in a tree and has a comfortable nest, but the rent is getting too high, so he is looking for a suitable flat mate. Various animals present themselves but none will do, until the perfect partner comes along – a lady bird, of course, complete with Easter bonnet.

2. *A Bird of Paradise:* To make a more exotic bird, alter the tail and give it long sweeping feathers. Elaborate upon the head crest, using your imagination to the full.

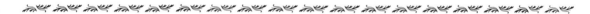

BOUNCY BIRD

Materials

2 identical wooden spoons, thick card; white undercoat; orange enamel; 18-in square purple felt; 6-in square emerald green felt; scraps of orange, black and white felt; 3 dress weights, 1-in diameter; kapok to stuff.

To Make

PREPARATION OF THE SPOON: Cut off the handle of one spoon so that the spoon measures $8\frac{1}{2}$ in from the tip of the bowl to the sawn off end of the handle. Drill two holes from side to side of the spoon handle to support the wings. These must be parallel with the bowl and should be bored $1\frac{1}{2}$ in and $3\frac{1}{2}$ in from the sawn off handle end.

TO PREPARE THE HEAD: Paint each spoon back and bowl first with undercoat and then with orange enamel, leaving the handle bare. Cut off the handle which has no holes bored in it just below the bowl of the spoon. The remaining painted part will form the bird's lower beak.

Stick one end of a 2 in by $\frac{5}{8}$ in strip of purple felt to the sawn off end of the lower beak spoon and fasten it down firmly with a small wood screw. See fig 121 in the instructions for the dragon. Fit the two spoon bowls together and stick the other end of the felt to the handle of the spoon. Wind it firmly round with thread to hold it in place. Stick another strip of orange felt to the inside of the bowls to strengthen the first hinge.

Hold the bowls exactly together with a rubber band and drill a small hole in the upper beak at the centre front, $\frac{1}{2}$ in from the edge, and a corresponding one through the lower beak. These will take the string which controls the bird's beak.

BODY: Cut a piece of purple felt for the body following the squared diagram on page 68. Run some adhesive down the centre of the spoon handle and lay this part along the felt body from A to B, having $\frac{1}{2}$ in of felt extending at B below the handle as shown in fig 99. Stick the end A to overlap the upper beak spoon bowl. Fold B over to hide the sawn off end of the handle and pleat the surplus felt together, then oversew B to C together on both sides of the body.

For the body front, cut a triangle of purple felt following the actual size pattern. Pin point C on the front to the lower point C on the body and sew from C to D on either side

67

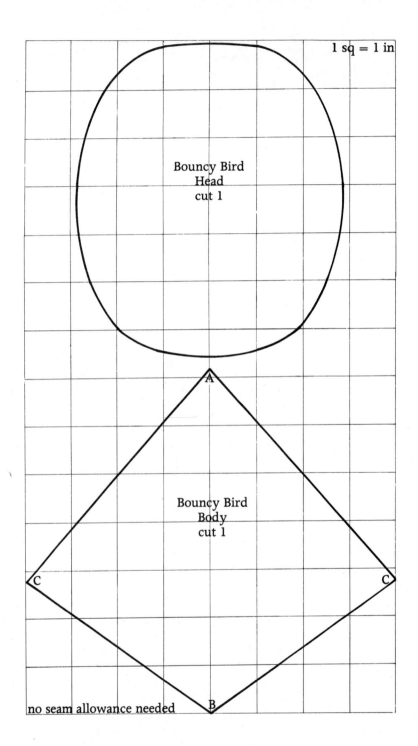

1 sq = 1 in

Bouncy Bird
Head
cut 1

Bouncy Bird
Body
cut 1

no seam allowance needed

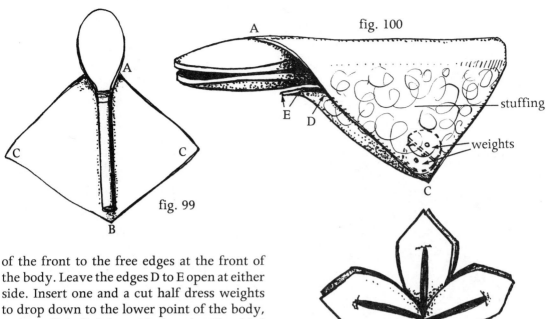

fig. 100

fig. 99

of the front to the free edges at the front of the body. Leave the edges D to E open at either side. Insert one and a cut half dress weights to drop down to the lower point of the body, and stuff it lightly with kapok. The bird should now look like fig 100.

HEAD: Cut the shape for the head in purple felt following the squared diagram on page 68. Run a gathering thread round the outside edges and draw it up to make an oval 2 in long by $1\frac{1}{2}$ in wide. Fasten off the gathering thread and stuff the head with kapok well pressed down. Apply adhesive to the surface of the kapok and to the gathered felt edge for about $\frac{1}{4}$ in outwards, and stick the head to the upper beak spoon, holding it in place with rubber bands while it dries. The position of the head on the spoon can vary a little, but see the illustration for a rough idea.

CREST: Cut 4 large emerald feathers, following the actual size pattern, and 2 orange ones. Stick two emerald feathers in a triangle to overlap the central orange one. Then stick the other two emerald feathers and the last orange one to the backs of the first three. With 6 strands of black stranded cotton or other thick black embroidery thread take a straight stitch along the centre of each feather. See fig 101. Stitch the crest to the bird's head.

TONGUE AND NOSTRILS: For nostrils, cut two black $\frac{1}{4}$-in diameter felt circles and stick

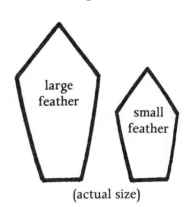

fig. 101

large feather

small feather

(actual size)

them to the upper beak on either side of the drilled hole. The tongue is a strip of black felt, 3 in long by $\frac{3}{4}$ in wide, tapered at one end. Stick inside the lower beak.

fig. 102

EYES: Cut two black eye backings and pupils and two white eyes from the actual size pattern and sew them one over the other following fig 102. Take a few white stitches for highlights on the pupils. Sew the eyes to the sides of the head. The position of the pupils can be varied to give the bird different expressions.

fig. 103

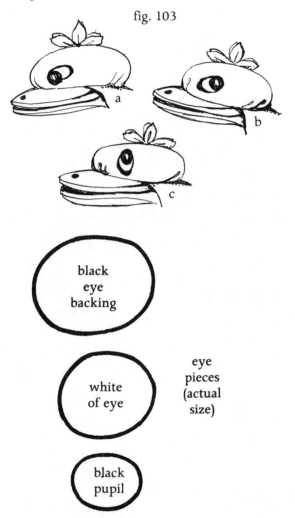

black
eye
backing

eye
pieces
(actual
size)

white
of eye

black
pupil

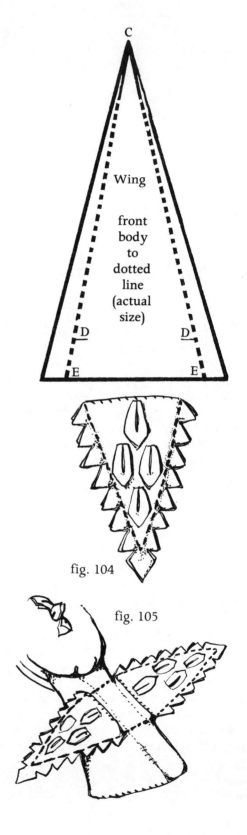

C

Wing

front
body
to
dotted
line
(actual
size)

D   D
E   E

fig. 104

fig. 105

WINGS: Cut two wings from stiff card following the actual size pattern given by unbroken lines on this page. Stick each on purple felt and cut out, allowing a surplus of $\frac{1}{2}$ in all round the slanting sides only. Stick the other side of the card on the emerald felt and cut out to the same size as the purple layer.

With purple cotton oversew the straight base edges together along the card. With double black cotton stab stitch the layers of felt together along the slanting sides of the card. Cut the surplus edges of the felt into zig-zags with a point at the top of the card.

Sew the wings to the sides of the body pushing the needle through the two holes bored in the spoon so that the wings are now hinged together at two points. Cut 8 small feathers from orange felt. Stick 4 to each wing following fig. 104 on p. 70 and take a black stitch along the centre of each.

TAIL: Cut a piece of thick card 2 in by $\frac{1}{2}$ in and stick a cut half of a weight to one side at the end. Cover the tail with purple felt on both sides. Cut two large emerald feathers and one orange one. Stick and sew with a straight stitch in black stranded cotton to one end of the tail, so that the green feathers point outwards in a V and the orange one overlaps in the middle. See the illustration on p. 66. Oversew the other end of the tail to the end of the body so that it hinges up and down.

FEET: Cut feet from stiff card, following the actual size pattern, and stick a dress weight to each foot as indicated by the dotted circle line. Cover them on both sides with orange felt and sew to the bottom point of the body, pushing the needle through the holes in the weight. See fig. 106.

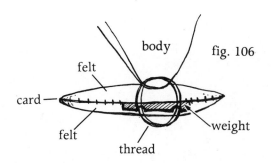

fig. 106

Control

MATERIALS: A 12-in strip of wood 1 in wide and an 8-in strip; small cup hook; length of round black elastic; button thread.

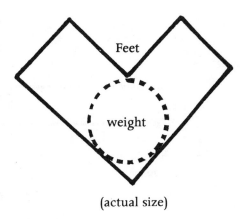

Feet

weight

(actual size)

TO MAKE: Insert a cup hook in one end of the 12-in strip. Glue and tie the 8-in strip at right angles to it, 6 in from the cup hook end. Cut nicks in the wood just before the cross bar and in the end opposite the cup hook. Cut nicks in the ends of the crossbar.

TO STRING: Find the point of balance by inserting a needle horizontally through the felt on top of the body and seeing if he will balance when you are holding him by the needle only. Probably this point will be just behind the head. With strong matching cotton stitched through the felt round the spoon handle sew the end of a length of round elastic to the balancing point of the body. This is string 1. Fasten the other end to the nicks in the wood just before the crossbar.

Tie a small bead to the end of a length of buttonholing thread for string 2 and thread it through the beak from the bottom. With the bird suspended by the elastic adjust the length so that the beak is open a little and pass the string through the cup hook. Tie another larger bead to this end so that the string can be removed from the cup hook at will to make the bird talk.

Sew string 3 to the tip of the tail and fasten it round the nicks in the other end of the main control, adjusting the length so that the tail slopes down slightly when the bird is hanging by the elastic. Take strings 4 and 5 from the

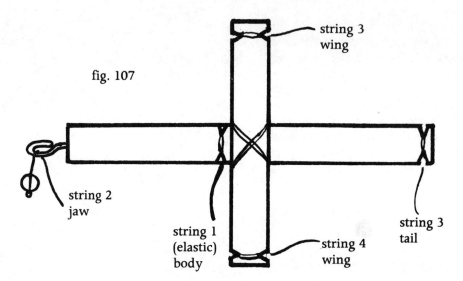

fig. 107

string 3
wing

string 2
jaw

string 1
(elastic)
body

string 4
wing

string 3
tail

wing tips to the ends of the crossbar, adjusting them so that the wings also hang down slightly.

TO OPERATE: The elastic makes the bird self-propelled in every respect. He can also perch on a branch and sing or talk.

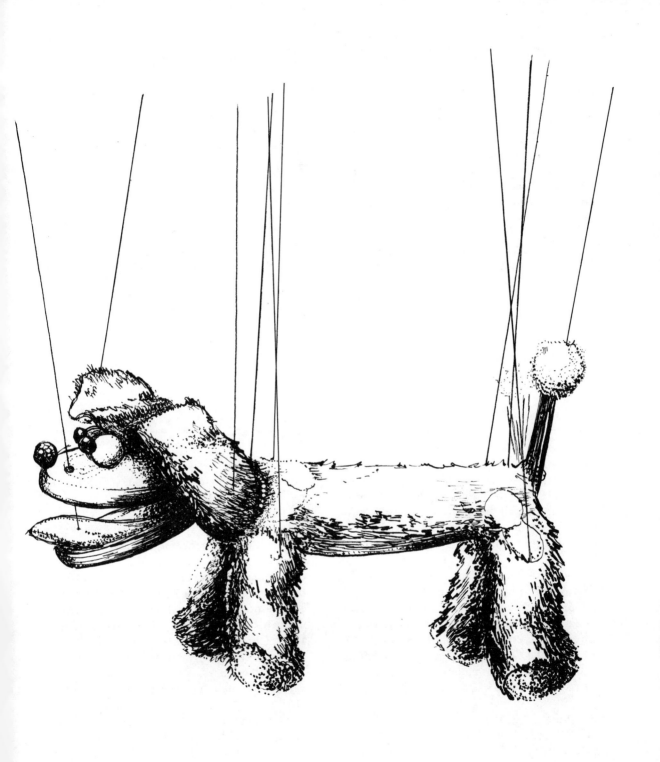

DOG WITH FLOPPY EARS

Although the stringing of the dog is a little more complicated than many of the other puppets, he is very rewarding to make and looks amusing. He can run along with no skill on the part of the operator and do many other tricks.

Variations

1. *A Different Dog:* As well as making him in different colours, you can alter his construction. Simplify his stringing by giving him legs like the dragon's, which are self operating. Alter his tail to one similar to the bouncy bird's. Eliminate his ear string and give him pointed, pricked up ears.

2. *A Comic Horse:* Make the legs about half as long again and alter the ears to triangular ones. Give him a mane and a longer tail. He won't look exactly like a horse, but enough like one to make people laugh.

3. *A Cat:* Make him in black and give him different ears and whiskers.

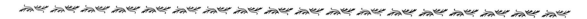

DOG WITH FLOPPY EARS

Materials

2 identical wooden spoons, preferably small ones; white undercoat; brown, tan and white enamel; 5 dress weights, 1-in diameter; thin string; small wood screw; piece of wood $\frac{3}{4}$ in wide by 3 in long by $\frac{1}{4}$ in thick, $1\frac{1}{2}$-in screw and small bead to thread on screw, last three items all for tail; $2\frac{3}{4}$-in square fur fabric (or use white felt), also for tail; 2 pieces $\frac{1}{4}$-in dowel about 1 in long; 1 matchstick; 1 round black bead about $\frac{3}{4}$ in diameter for nose; 2 round beads $\frac{5}{8}$ to $\frac{3}{4}$ in diameter in any colour to stuff eyes; 2 round black beads or black sequins each about $\frac{3}{8}$ in diameter also for eyes; piece brown fur fabric 9 in by 14 in with the pile running down the shorter sides; 9-in square tan felt; small pieces red and white felt; small amount of kapok; $\frac{1}{2}$ pipe cleaner.

To Make

PREPARATION OF THE SPOON: Cut off the handle of one of the spoons so that it now measures $5\frac{1}{2}$ in below the bowl, and drill small holes from side to side of the handle, parallel to the bowl, one $\frac{3}{4}$ in below it and one $1\frac{1}{4}$ in from the end. See fig 108. Drill a small

fig. 108

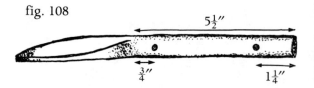

hole in the sawn-off end of the spoon to take the $1\frac{1}{2}$-in screw for the tail.

HEAD: Paint each spoon back and bowl with undercoat leaving the handle bare. Then paint the back of each spoon brown and the bowl red. When the enamel is dry paint white and tan patches at random on the top of the brown enamel of the spoon which has holes drilled in the handle, and paint a line of white enamel about $\frac{1}{4}$ in wide all round the edges of the red bowls of the spoons to represent teeth. Cut off the handle of the spoon which has no patches painted on it just below the bowl. This part is for the dog's lower jaw.
Stick one end of a 2 in by $\frac{5}{8}$ in strip of tan felt to the sawn off end of the lower jaw spoon and fasten it down firmly with a small wood screw. Fit the two spoon bowls together and stick the other end of felt to the handle of the second spoon. Wind it firmly round with thread to hold it in place. See fig 121 in the

instructions for the dragon. Stick another strip of red felt to the inside of the bowl to strengthen the first hinge.

fig. 109
Top spoon only

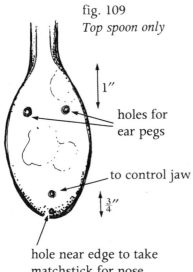

1″

holes for ear pegs

to control jaw

$\frac{3}{4}$″

hole near edge to take matchstick for nose

Following fig 109, drill two $\frac{1}{4}$-in diameter holes to fit the dowel pegs which support the ears in the top spoon only. The holes need not penetrate the wood. Drill a $\frac{1}{8}$-in hole in the centre tip of the spoon at a slight angle sloping inwards if possible. This will later take a matchstick on which you will glue the bead for the nose, and a tip tilted angle is more amusing.

Holding the upper and lower jaws together, drill a small hole through the upper jaw towards the centre front as indicated in fig 109, and a corresponding one through the lower jaw. These will take the string which controls the animal's mouth.

PREPARATION OF LEGS: Cut two lengths of fine string each about 24 in long and thread on a dress weight about 4 in from one end. Take the longer end through one of the holes in the spoon handle and thread on another dress weight. Push the string back through the same hole and adjust the length so that there are $10\frac{1}{2}$ in between the weights as shown in fig 110. Knot the ends of the strings securely and cut off surplus. Prepare the other pair of legs in the same way. Adjust

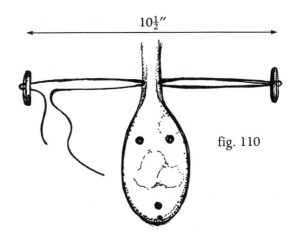

$10\frac{1}{2}$″

fig. 110

string so that all the legs are the same length and add dabs of glue to the strings where they pass through the holes so that they stay in place.

BODY: Cut a $3\frac{1}{4}$ in by $6\frac{1}{2}$ in strip of brown fur fabric for the dog's back with the pile running down the length, and a strip of tan felt for his tummy $1\frac{1}{4}$ in by $6\frac{1}{2}$ in. Take the fur fabric and running stitch or oversew $\frac{1}{4}$-in turning to the wrong side on two long sides and one short one.

Smear fabric adhesive lightly down the top of the spoon handle and stick the centre of the fur back along it so that the turned in short end comes just over the join of the spoon jaws and the raw end matches the sawn off end of the handle. Pin the tan felt to the edges of the fur allowing the string legs to hang outside. Oversew the felt to the fur back but leave the end of the body unsewn. Push in some kapok to pad it out. When you have completed the ears, use remaining tan felt to make random patches on body and legs.

fig. 111

LEGS: Cut 4 red circles each $1\frac{1}{4}$-in diameter from red felt and stick them on the lower surface of each weight for the paws. Cut 4 pieces of fur fabric each $3\frac{1}{2}$ in by $4\frac{1}{2}$ in with the pile running down the longer sides. Oversew the longer edges together and with the pile running downwards turn in the lower edges for $\frac{1}{4}$ in and oversew or running stitch them to hold them down. Turn work to right side.

Slip one tube on to the string and weight inner leg so that the turned in edge is next to the paw. Oversew these two together all round. Fold the top flat and stitch it to the body (see figs 112 and 113). Lay the dog on its back and stitch the inside of the leg to the edge of the tummy. Complete each leg in the same way.

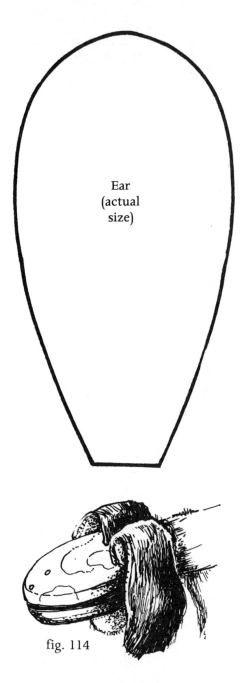

Ear
(actual
size)

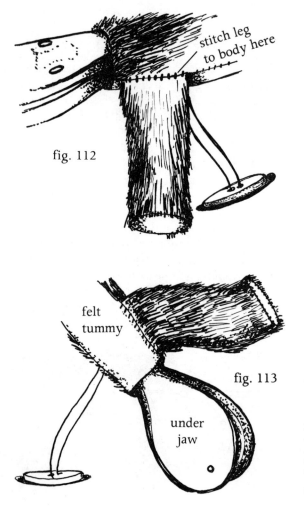

fig. 112

fig. 113

fig. 114

EARS: Stick the dowels into the holes in the head, using wood glue. From the actual size pattern cut two ears in fur fabric with the pile running down and two in tan felt. Oversew the pairs together with wrong sides facing, leaving the straight base edges open. Cut a weight in half and apply a little adhesive to one side. Slip half into each ear, dropping it right down to the end. Apply plenty of adhesive to each dowel peg and slip the ears over them, so that the tan inside of each ear faces inwards and the ears flop down over the sides of the head.

EYES: For each eye cut a circle of white felt $1\frac{3}{4}$-in diameter and run a gathering thread round the outside. Place a $\frac{3}{4}$-in diameter bead in the centre of the circle and pull up the thread tightly to enclose it, or stuff the felt firmly to a ball. Make the other eye in the same way. With the gathering underneath sew a $\frac{3}{8}$-in diameter black bead or sequin to one side of the felt for the pupils, so that the eyes are near enough together in a squint, though you may vary this as you please.

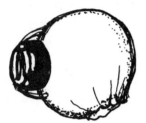

fig. 115

Roughen a patch just in front of the ears and glue the eyes to it, sticking the insides of the eyes together. See fig 116.

NOSE: Sharpen a piece of match stick so that it can be glued into the $\frac{1}{2}$-in diameter black bead for the nose, and stick the rest of the match stick into the hole already drilled.

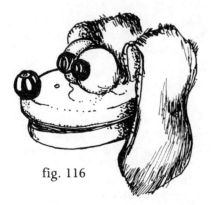

fig. 116

TONGUE: Cut two tongues from red felt from the actual size pattern and stick a piece of pipe cleaner down the centre length of one of them. Oversew the tongues together, padding lightly with kapok as you sew, and stick the back of the tongue into the lower jaw so that the tip protrudes for about $\frac{1}{2}$ in and the tongue can be arched slightly by bending the pipe cleaner.

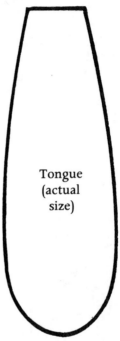

Tongue (actual size)

TAIL: Shape the long edges of the wood for the tail with a penknife, sandpaper or a wood file so that they are curved, and curve the corners of one short end. Drill a hole big enough to pivot easily round the $1\frac{1}{2}$-in long screw, situated centrally $\frac{1}{2}$-in from the

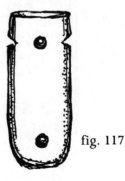

fig. 117

curved short end. Drill a similar hole in the other end, and cut nicks in the side of the wood on a line with the hole. Paint the tail with white undercoat and then with brown enamel.

Cut a circle of white fur fabric 2¾-in diameter and run a gathering thread round the outside. Insert a little kapok and draw up the thread so that it fits round the nicked end of the wood. Attach the fabric firmly to the wood by means of the nicks and the drilled hole. Insert a 1½-in screw through the hole at the other end of the tail and thread on the bead, then drive the screw firmly into the hole drilled in the tail end of the spoon handle.

Run a gathering thread round the end of the body and pull it up well to enclose the spoon handle. Paint the end of the screw brown or stick a scrap of fur fabric over it to hide it.

Control

MATERIALS: One 15-in strip of wood 1 in wide and three 8-in strips; 1 small cup hook; a 1-in long dowel peg, ¼-in diameter; 7-in length round elastic, any colour, 1 small and 1 large bead; button thread.

TO MAKE: Insert a cup hook into one end of the 15-in strip of wood and drill a hole to fit the peg 2½ in from this end. Drill a hole to fit comfortably over the peg in the centre of one crossbar.

Cut nicks for strings 5 in and 9½ in away from the cup hook end, in the opposite end of the

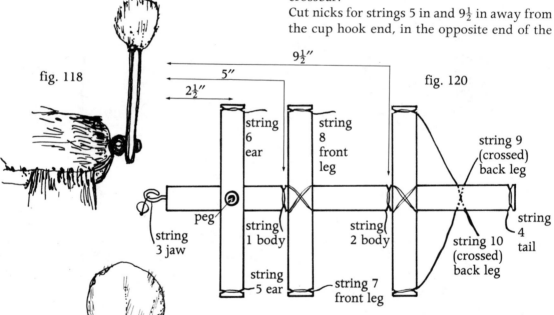

fig. 118

fig. 120

fig. 119

9½″

5″

2½″

string 6 ear

string 8 front leg

string 9 (crossed) back leg

peg

string 3 jaw

string 1 body

string 2 body

string 10 (crossed) back leg

string 4 tail

string 5 ear

string 7 front leg

main strip and in the ends of each crossbar. Glue and bind the two undrilled crossbars at right angles to the main strip 5¼ in and 9¾ in away from the cup hook end, just behind the nicks. Glue the peg in place.

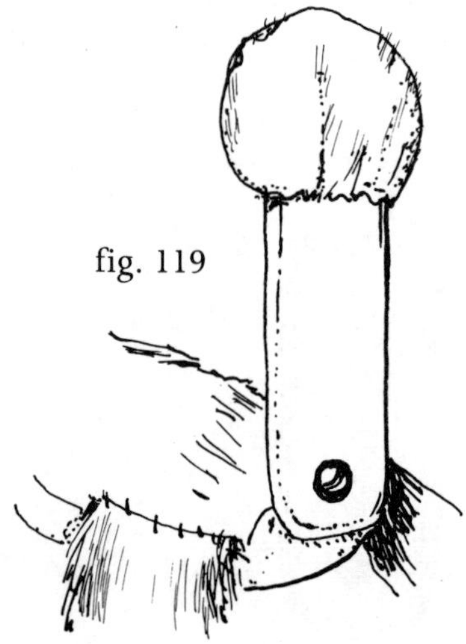

TO STRING: Sew string 1 firmly into the dog just behind his head and take it to the nicks 5 inches along the control. Attach string 2 from the end of the body 1 inch in front of the tail to the nicks 9½ in along the control. String 3 runs from the holes in the jaw to the cup hook in the front of the control. Tie a small bead to the end underneath the jaw and a large one to the end going through the hook, and adjust the length so that the jaw remains slightly open. Securely fasten a loop of round elastic to the nicks at the other end of the control and take string 4 from the tip of the tail through the elastic loop. Adjust the length so that the tail stands up.

To operate the ears, take strings 5 and 6 from their tips, stitching through the dress weights if possible, to the ends of the front crossbar. Sew strings 7 and 8 to the outside of the front legs, about half way down each, and take the other ends to the middle crossbar.

The back legs are strung differently. To make sure that the dog lifts the rear leg on the opposite side at the same time as he lifts a front leg the strings should be crossed. String 9 will run from the outside of a back leg to the end of the back crossbar on the other side, and string 10 is arranged in the same way.

TO OPERATE: To walk the dog, rock the control rapidly from side to side while moving him along. The ears will rise and fall as well. If you want to keep them still, or prick them independently, remove the crossbar from the peg on the main control and hold it in your other hand. Make him sit on his hind legs and beg, or lift his ears while he pants with his mouth open. Remove the bead from the cup hook to work the mouth without moving the rest of the body. Tilt the control forwards to make him crouch on his front legs while you jerk the piece of elastic to wag his tail.

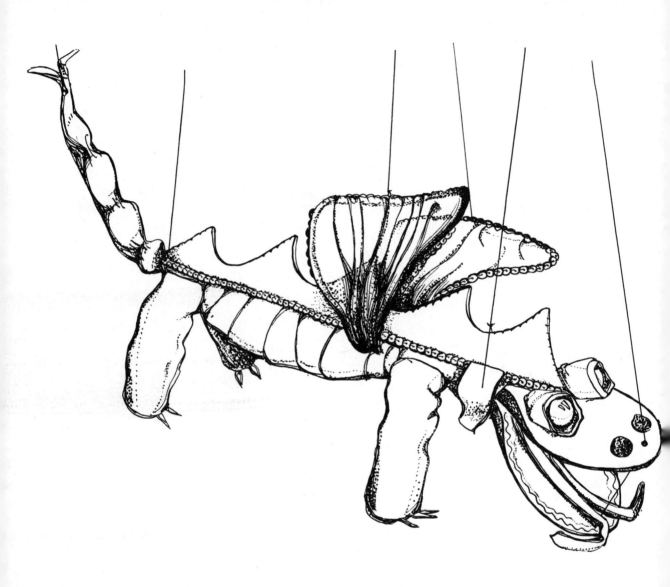

DRAGON

This is an animal puppet with self-operating legs. They bounce up and down of their own accord on weighted hair rollers. Wings flutter and tail lashes to make a fully mobile monster.

Variations

1. *A Dinosaur:* Choose the largest wooden spoons you can find. There are wooden ladles from Portugal in some shops. Alternatively, make papier mâché moulds over a metal soup ladle or a small oval casserole. Grease the ladle first and then stick layers of torn newspaper over it with wallpaper paste. About ten layers should make a strong construction. Fasten a dowel rod inside one of the shapes with wire and pasted newspaper for the back bone. Alter the other measurements accordingly.

2. *A Baby Dragon:* Make this on small spoons. Write a play about a baby dragon who hatched from an egg the bouncy bird had in her nest. The first dragon can be very tiny, on one string only, then he grows a bit into the small one, then into the full-sized one and finally into the dinosaur. Meanwhile the bouncy bird is having a terrible time trying to feed him. For the ending, she can either make her fortune hiring him as a secret weapon/a pollution pet in the government's latest drive to devour rubbish/a heating element for the bird's swimming pool.

3. *A Dragon with different legs:* Alter his leg design to those of the dog with floppy ears.

DRAGON

Materials

2 identical wooden spoons; white undercoat; green and red enamel; the springs from four 1-in diameter hair rollers; 5–9 dress weights, 1-in diameter; 15 pipe cleaners, green ones if possible; metallic ric-rac, gold paper, sequins, braid etc, to decorate; two marbles for eyes; scraps red felt and card, green and red lurex material.

To Make

PREPARATION OF THE SPOON: Drill four holes in the handle of one of the spoons $\frac{1}{2}$ in, $1\frac{1}{2}$ in, 8 in and 7 in from the end. These holes support the legs and must be drilled from side to side of the handle, parallel with the bowl of the spoon.

fig. 121a

HEAD: Paint each spoon bowl and back with undercoat, leaving the handle bare. Then paint the bowl of each spoon red and the back green.

When the paint is dry cut off the handle which has no holes bored in it just below the bowl of the spoon. The remaining painted part will form the dragon's lower jaw. Stick one end of a 2 in by $\frac{5}{8}$ in strip of red felt to the sawn-off end of the spoon and anchor it down firmly with a small wood screw; fit the two spoon bowls together and stick the other end of felt to the handle of the second spoon; wind it firmly round with thread to hold it in place. Stick another strip of red felt to the inside of the bowl to strengthen the first hinge.

fig. 121b

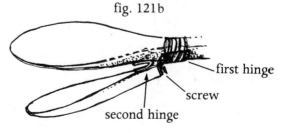

first hinge

screw

second hinge

Drill a small hole through the upper jaw towards the top centre, and a corresponding hole through the lower jaw. These will take the string which controls the mouth.

Wind a strip of red felt into a cone shape and stick a marble inside it with impact adhesive for an eye. Place the red felt cone inside a slightly larger cone of gold paper. Make another eye in the same way and stick them to the top of the upper jaw. Cut two strips of green material and stick them to the top of each eye for a wrinkled eyelid. The nostrils

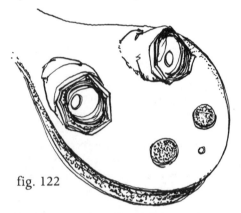

fig. 122

are two small circles of red felt stuck down with adhesive. Glue silver ric-rac braid to the inside of the top and bottom jaws for teeth. Make a forked tongue from 10-in pipe cleaner covered with red lurex material and stick it inside the lower jaw, allowing it to protrude a little in front.

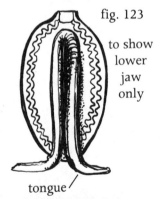

fig. 123

to show lower jaw only

tongue

BODY: Bind the handle of the spoon firmly with a strip of green lurex material, covering the rounded end of the handle and the felt hinge.

LEGS: Take each wire hair roller spring and pull the coils a little apart to make them more springy. Bend each spring over in a curve. Cut off the last two or three coils from each to shorten them a little and thread one or two lead weights on the cut ends so that the springs will bounce up and down. Secure the weights by bending over the spring ends; add a little glue and wind thread round the wire if necessary. Make four tubes of green lurex

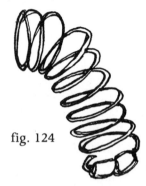

fig. 124

material to cover the springs; tuck the raw edges inside the unweighted ends and over-sew them to the wire; oversew a circle of red felt to the raw edges of the tubes on each weighted end. Add three or four gold sequins to each foot for claws.

ATTACHING THE LEGS: Sew the legs in pairs firmly to the body through the holes which you have drilled, passing the thread round the top ring of each spring.

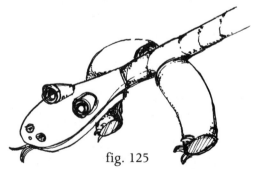

fig. 125

Sew two small strips of green lurex on top of the body, from side to side on the back and front pairs of legs, so that you hide the holes. A close-up is shown in fig 126. Make sure that you use sufficient material to allow the legs to curve over as they were when you attached them.

extra piece of lurex

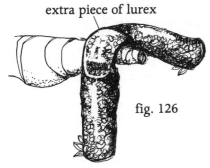

fig. 126

UNDERBODY: Pad the underneath of the spoon handle between the legs with a little kapok or cotton wool and hold it in place with thread. Cut a strip of red lurex material and wind it round the padding to give the effect of a paunchy stomach.

WINGS: Take two pipe cleaners and twist the ends together for about 1 in. Do the same twice more with four more pipe cleaners.

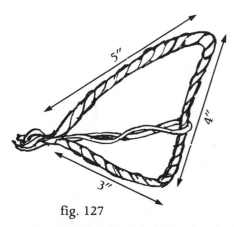

fig. 127

Twist the three double lengths together, then bend them into the wing shape shown in fig 127. Fold one pipe cleaner in half over the top of the triangle and twist it round the lower point where all the ends meet. Cut a piece of red and a piece of green lurex material each $6\frac{1}{2}$ in by $4\frac{1}{2}$ in. Pin them together, right sides facing, and gather along one lower edge; pull up to measure 4 in. Turn the work to the right side; slip the pipe cleaner frame in between them, and sew the gathering to the top of the wing triangle. Pleat most of the

other long edge in to the meeting point of the pipe cleaners; then sew the short edges to the other two edges of the wing triangle, trimming away any surplus material. Stick sequin banding all round the outside and down the centre where the single pipe cleaner forms a rib.

fig. 128

Prepare the other wing in the same way, then sew the wings to either side of the dragon's back about 1 in behind the front legs, using surplus material at the point of the triangles as hinges so that the wings can be flapped up and down.

TAIL: Cut one triangle each of red and green lurex, about 2 in wide at the base by 6 in long. With right sides facing sew the sloping sides together. Turn to right side. Slip a weight into the pointed end and lightly stuff the rest.

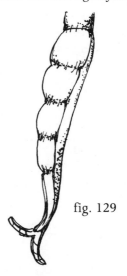

fig. 129

Work four rows of running stitches 1 in apart across the width of the tail and draw up slightly to give the effect of segments. Turn the raw edges to the inside and sew the tail to the tip of the spoon handle. Cut a 2-in length of pipe cleaner and cover it with red material. Sew it to the end of the tail for a forked tip.

BACK SPINE: Take a strip of card 11 in by $1\frac{1}{2}$ in, and cut one long side into 5 curved spikes. Cover each side of the card with red felt, allowing $\frac{1}{4}$-in surplus along the straight edges which will be used later to attach the spine to the dragon. Oversew the felt edges together along the curves and take a line of running stitches along the straight edge,

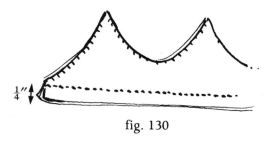

fig. 130

close to the card. Open out the $\frac{1}{4}$-in surplus felt pieces and pin these along the centre of the dragon's back; the spine will reach along the head between the eyes. Stick the extension to the dragon's head and stitch the felt to the back along the edges. Stick sequin banding over the stitching at either side of the spine. To hide the join of the lower jaw to the upper, cut two pieces of felt each $1\frac{3}{4}$ in by 1 in and round off one corner of each. Stick a piece to each side of the spine, over the sequin banding, just behind the head, as shown in fig 131.

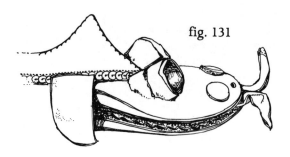

fig. 131

Control

MATERIALS: 15-in strip of 1-in wide wood; 2 small cup hooks; 2 small screw eyes; 1 small and 2 large beads; button thread.

TO MAKE: Insert a small cup hook into each end of the wood and a small screw eye into each side of it 5 in from one end. Hold the wood so that the screw eyes are towards the left and mark along $2\frac{1}{2}$ in and $11\frac{1}{2}$ in from the left hand end. Cut nicks either side at the marks.

TO STRING: Take string 1 from a point on the back spine just behind the head and tie it round the nick $2\frac{1}{2}$ in away from the left. String 2 is sewn into the other end of the spoon handle and tied round the other nicks. For string 3, take a length of thread from the holes in the jaw through the appropriate end hook. Tie a small bead on the end underneath the jaw and a large bead on the end going through the hook so that it will remain in place and can easily be removed for operation. Run string 4 from the tip of the tail through the second end hook with a bead at the hook end. Strings 5 and 6 are in one continuous length from each wing tip through the screw eyes, with a large bead tied in the centre so

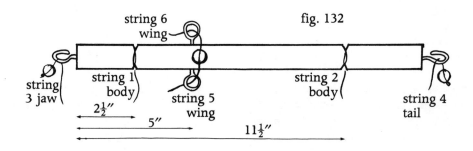

fig. 132

string 6 wing

string 3 jaw

string 1 body

$2\frac{1}{2}''$

$5''$

string 5 wing

$11\frac{1}{2}''$

string 2 body

string 4 tail

that they can easily be picked up. Adjust the length so that the wings are slightly lifted.

TO OPERATE: Move the control up and down to make the legs bounce, or rest the back legs on the floor and shake the front of the control to make the jaw clap, the wings flutter and the tail move. Wave the end of the control from side to side to lash the tail, or flap the wings by shaking it up and down when the rest of the dragon is stationary. The dragon can also be made to clash his jaws in a roar by removing the bead on string 3 and jerking it.

PUPPET THEATRES

As soon as you have made one or two puppets you will want some kind of theatre for them. Many books will give instructions for elaborate marionette theatres but it is not necessary to go to such trouble before you can present a show before an audience.

It is perfectly possible to operate your puppets without a theatre of any kind. Many orientals work in this way. The audience watches the puppets, not you. Just wear something dark which will form a good background for the costumes. You can stand on a low table or some other kind of platform which will raise you a little.

If you want to use any kind of scenery you will need a simple theatre. This will need the minimum of a back drop and front wings in some form or another, and must be open at the top to allow for the strings. Additions would be some form of upper screen which covers the top half of the puppeteers, and a rail or some hooks behind the theatre on which you can hang the puppets before they make their entrances.

1. Any kind of doors centrally situated in a room would make a good marionette theatre. Let your audience in first. Then turn a table on its side. Put the table about 18 in behind the doorway and cover the front with a back cloth. The puppets enter from behind the sides of the door. These are the wings. You could hang another cloth from a rail at the top of the doorway to hide your upper halves from the audience, or drawing pin it in place. See fig 133.

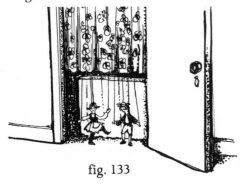

fig. 133

2. If you have no convenient doorway, you can still use a table on its side for the backdrop. If you can rig up some kind of curtain which will hide your top half, so much the better, but this may be difficult. Impromptu wings may be tall thin boxes standing on end, or if these are not sufficiently stable stick a strut of cardboard at the back. Let the boxes lean over slightly, to make sure they do not fall over at the wrong moment. Cover them with fancy paper or paint them. Alternatively, the wings can be made from sheets of hardboard with struts at the back.

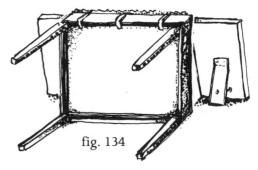

fig. 134

3. If you can do simple woodwork, or can get help, you can make a simple portable theatre from flat strips of wood and hardboard. The back drop is a piece of hardboard with two or three hinged struts at the back to prop it up. If the hardboard bends too much, nail strips of wood round the outside. The wings are two pieces of hardboard supported by struts and joined by strips of wood at top and bottom. You can hang front stage curtains from the upper strip. For simple drape curtains you will need at least one and a half times the width of the stage opening in curtain material, 2 large screw eyes, drawing pins, small curtain rings and cord. Sew curtain rings diagonally to wrong side of curtain making sure you have a pair (see fig 135). Attach top of curtains to the inside of the stage opening with drawing pins. Insert screw eyes where indicated. Attach a string to the lowest ring on each curtain and thread through remaining rings. Note that the string

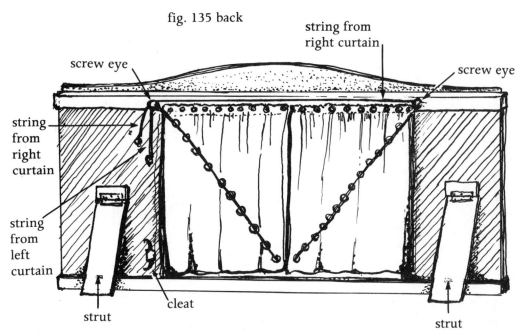

fig. 135 back

string from
right curtain

screw eye

screw eye

string
from
right
curtain

string
from
left
curtain

cleat

strut

strut

from the right-hand curtain goes through the right-hand screw eye, across the top of the stage and then through the left-hand screw eye. The left-hand string goes through the left-hand screw eye only. This makes it possible to manipulate both curtains with one hand. Wind strings round a cleat when the curtains are raised. The advantage of this theatre is that it will fold flat for storage.

the other end right away so that the top is completely open. Cut the smaller sides right away except for the bottom 3 or 4 inches. You will now have a box without any top and with only enough sides to hold front and back together. Cut the stage opening in one side, leaving the flap intact. Leave the other side uncut for the back drop. Strengthen the front and back if necessary with pieces of card cut from another box stuck in place.

fig. 136 front

fig. 137

4. You can have fun making a theatre from a large cardboard packing case, the biggest you can get. See if you can beg one from a shop, and another smaller one if possible, to use for strengthening. Select the end which has the flaps most intact and cut the flaps from

When you are using the theatre the bottom flaps will stay open to steady the whole thing. If it is not sufficiently stable you could glue pieces of card between the front and back and each flap at the ends, as shown in fig 138.

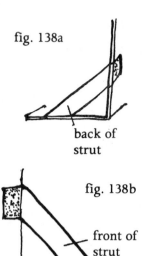

fig. 138a

back of strut

fig. 138b

front of strut

SCENERY AND PROPS

It is a great mistake to make scenery which is at all realistic. Often the best background is a perfectly plain piece of material or paper. Anything too detailed will compete with the costumes of the puppets to make too busy an effect. Sometimes, however, a performance calls for one or two scenic additions. When designing them remember that puppets cannot do anything which will interfere with their strings, such as coming through doorways or windows, unless the opening is cut right to the top of the scene. Keep all scenery as simple as possible in outline and colour. Use flat tones and do not give any perspective. The impact will be much greater and more stylized.

You may make cut-outs from strong card which can be slotted into a flat support of a piece of wood, to stand freely, or hung by

fig. 139a

fig. 139b

threads and hooks from the top of the stage back. You can also paint the whole scene on to a sheet of strong paper. Drawing pin a batten (a strip of wood) to the top and bottom of the sheet to prevent tearing, and screw hooks into the batten at the top to hang the scene over the stage back. The scenery may be rolled when not in use; the batten at the bottom will weight the paper so that the curl given by rolling the scene will drop out.

fig. 140

It is often very effective to cut apertures in the scenery, such as windows or spaces between the branches of the trees, so that the puppets can appear behind them to give more interest to their movements on the stage. In this case the scenery will have to be free standing, as anything hanging from the space at the top of the stage would interfere with the manipulation of the strings. Instead of painted back drops, you may like to cut shapes from fabric and stick or stitch them to large plain pieces of material to hang at the back of the stage. Brown tweed tree trunks with large felt leaves would look very bold and make more impact than the same shapes painted. Use of the scissors necessitates simplicity of outline, and this is all to the good. You could also try cutting the same shape twice with a seam allowance. Place right sides together and stitch round leaving a space unsewn, turn to right side and stuff lightly. Pin the scenery on to a back cloth and hang this with hooks over the back of the stage. The stuffing gives a pleasing three-dimensional effect.

fig. 141

Other pieces of scenery can grow, for instance the beanstalk in *Jack, the Giant Killer,* or you might centre a plot round a prize flower that grew larger and larger. Start with a heavily weighted base. The stalk may be round elastic, with felt leaves attached at intervals. Fix strings to each side of the flat flower head and run them to the ends of a straight strip of wood for a control at the top. Screw a large cup hook at each end of the control. When you have stretched up the flower to its full height you can hang the hooks over the top of the back stage. Alternatively, make the weighted

pot hollow and stitch the leaves to a length of green cord for a stalk. Coil the stalk inside the pot and draw it slowly out and upwards by means of the control attached to the top of the flower.

fig. 142

Use the same idea for a snake sliding from its basket to dance before a snake charmer, a genie coming out of a bottle, or the sun coming up over a hill. Any other pieces of scenery such as a table or chairs should not have projecting pieces in case the strings of the puppets become entangled, and if any thing is put on them, such as a vase on a table, it should be fastened down in case it is knocked off during a performance.

LIGHTING

If you can arrange some simple form of lighting your performance is made more theatrical. The simplest and easiest way is to position an anglepoise lamp at the side of the stage, or better still two, one at either side. You may also be able to fix an adjustable wall light, like a small spot light, behind each of your side screens. More simply, bicycle lights could be used.

SUGGESTIONS FOR A VARIETY SHOW

After you have created your theatre, you will want to put on some kind of show. This could consist of some or all of the following items.
1. The Expanding Clown, who tells jokes and riddles, tap dances and does acrobatics.
2. The Fairy or the Fat Old King, wearing a top hat, who brings in the amazing performing dog.
3. The Pop Singer.
4. Hansel and Gretel, who dance.
5. A short play.
The last item can be a dramatized version of any traditional fairy story, such as *Hansel and Gretel, Cinderella, The Sleeping Beauty* or *The Tinder Box*. You could also act many long poems, particularly those of Edward Lear or Hilaire Belloc. For instance the poem from Hilaire Belloc's *Cautionary Tales* about Matilda, a little girl who liked to pretend there was a fire in her house until one day there really was one, could be narrated by the Queen with Gretel as the little girl in the story.

The puppets in this book can be modified by slight additions to their costumes, or the instructions can be altered to make other puppets as described in the basic instructions and in the introduction to each puppet.

A combination of the characters in the book will suggest a situation which can be developed into a play. Two ideas follow to set your imagination working. Either write lines for them or make up words as you go along, but practise with your partners beforehand.

If you are reading the lines you will have to hang a copy of them clipped together at the top on hooks, one on either side of the stage, or you could pre-record them on a tape recorder. Alter the plays or change them as suits you and the number of people there are to help. You need one pair of hands to work each puppet, unless you can hang one or more puppets on a rod over the stage while they are not supposed to be joining in the action.

The puppets described in this book can be used for the plays suggested below. Variations of the puppets are given in the introduction to each one.

THE WITCH WHO CHANGED HER MIND

Characters

Fairy, Witch, Bird, Cat (another version of the Dog with Floppy Ears), Dragon, Doctor (Fat Old King).

SCENE 1: The witch arrives on a broomstick to have tea with her sister who is a fairy. The fairy sits down but says she doesn't want much, she's already eaten nearly all the cakes and jelly before the teaparty and now she's been so greedy she can feel a tummy ache coming on. Soon she feels so ill she has to go to bed. In comes the doctor with a huge black bag (attach it to his hand with a safety pin or sew a large eye to his hand and a hook to the bag). After a consultation he says he'll have to give her an injection. He goes out to get his hypodermic syringe which is also huge. After all the skirmishing the doctor departs and the witch re-enters to tuck the fairy up in bed and tell her not to worry, she will look after everything while the fairy gets better, and in any case it has been her life's ambition to be good at last. She summons her faithful black cat and the fairy calls for her bird, and each is asked to be helpful.

SCENE 2: The fairy has been ill for a week and is in bed asleep. The witch says the fairy isn't recovering and she cannot understand it. She asks the cat who says he has been feeding the fairy well with all the nice things the witch likes such as bat stew, worm pie and fried slugs, and by now she should be feeling much better. So the witch rushes off to the nearest supermarket to buy something much

more suitable. The fairy wakes up and says she's so hungry she'll just have to eat something instead of throwing it all through the window, and gulps down a jar of pickled toadstools which is standing on her bedside table. She asks the cat what he's been eating as he looks so well, and then wonders where her bird is. At last she suspects the cat who is so guilty he begins to whistle. He begs to be forgiven and says he really is so good nowadays, his fairy bird meal has quite changed his character.

SCENE 3: One week later. The witch is quite tipsy on yet another bottle of fairy wine and is wearing a fairy crown in a haphazard fashion and carrying a wand. (Make a crown in a three quarter circle and put it round the witch's hat.) She calls to the cat who comes in flying and whistling like a bird. The fairy flies in on the witch's broomstick wearing her sister's second best hat (make it open at the back and drop it over the fairy's head string) and a tattered cloak. She's eaten all the witch's food and is having a great time being bad, and is not a bit sorry about her boring old bird who would have eaten all her tastiest worms anyway. In fact, she's bought a much better pet, which has just been delivered in a huge box at the back of the stage.

She's going to make a splendid career of being a witch and will do things in style. She bangs on the side of the box. Loud roarings are heard and out springs the dragon who chases the witch and her cat off the stage.

THE DRAGON WHO WOULDN'T

Characters

Fat Old King, Fat Old Queen, Beautiful Princess (either Gretel or Fairy), Handsome Prince (Pop Singer), Ghost, Dragon.

SCENE 1: The king and queen are bemoaning modern goings-on and young people in general. They decide to return to the good old days and give their only daughter to whoever can slay the dragon they hear now lives in the wood. They call for the princess who is not at all pleased. She says her boyfriend is really a Prince, but now he's gone to live in a commune and practise the guitar and can she marry him if he slays the dragon. He could do with a spot of ready cash and marrying her will be just the answer. She makes such a fuss that in the end the king and queen let her ring him on the telephone/hang out a banner/dispatch a message by the bouncy bird who has taken over since the last postal strike, and he comes in to receive his instructions.

SCENE 2: The prince is outside the dragon's cave. It's no good; he must have a rest. He drops off to sleep. The ghost emerges from the cave. Great gibbering skeletons, here's another of them come to interfere with his friend the dragon who only asks for a quiet life: he'll have to frighten this one off too. Loud moanings are heard, accompanied by much arm waving. The prince wakes up.

Far from being frightened, he is fascinated by the ghost's up to the minute chain jewellery and smart cut of his winding sheet, the slimming went a bit too far but never mind about that. The prince is all for peace and love really, so could he just have the dragon's autograph and then he thinks he had better be getting back, the princess will be worrying. The dragon emerges from the cave. He is frightened at first but soon makes friends.

SCENE 3: We are back at the court. In comes the prince leading the dragon. He tells the queen and king there won't be any dragon slaying, and in any case he and the dragon have taken a great fancy to each other and have decided to form a group along with the ghost who can do a neat percussion job of chain rattling. The king and queen say all right, they suppose they must move with the times, and the princess is overjoyed at her parents' permission to marry the prince and says she has always longed to be the lead singer in a group. They end with a song, the prince plays his guitar, the ghost rattles his chains like maraccas, and the dragon strikes a triangle/drum/xylophone with his tail, while the princess sings and her parents dance.